Advanced Pathfinder 5
Getting to grips with grammar

Other titles in the series

Learning through listening (Advanced Pathfinder 6)
Helen Wright

Managing coursework (Advanced Pathfinder 4)
Colin Christie

Tests and targets (Advanced Pathfinder 3)
Ted Neather

Developing learning strategies (Advanced Pathfinder 2)
Barry Jones

Advancing oral skills (Advanced Pathfinder 1)
Anneli McLachlan

CiLT The National Centre for Languages

CILT, the National Centre for Languages, seeks to support and develop multilingualism and intercultural competence among all sectors of the population in the UK.

CILT is a registered charity, supported by Central Government grants.

advAnced Pathfinder

5

Getting to grips with grammar

TED NEATHER

CiLT The National Centre for Languages

The views expressed in this publication are the author's and do not necessarily represent those of CILT.

Acknowledgements

The author and publisher would like to thank copyright holders for the permission granted to reproduce copyright material, as detailed next to the relevant excerpts.

In some cases it has not been possible to trace copyright holders of material reproduced in this book. The publisher will be pleased to make the appropriate arrangement with any copyright holder whom it has not been possible to contact at the earliest opportunity.

First published 2003 by the Centre for Information on Language Teaching and Research (CILT), 20 Bedfordbury, London, WC2N 4LB

Copyright © Centre for Information on Language Teaching and Research 2003

ISBN 1 904243 09 6

A catalogue record for this book is available from the British Library

Ted Neather has asserted his right to be identified as author of this work, in accordance with the Copyright, Designs and Patents Act, 1988.

Printed in Great Britain by Hobbs

CILT Publications are available from: **Central Books**, 99 Wallis Rd, London E9 5LN. Tel: 0845 458 9910. Fax: 0845 458 9912. Book trade representation (UK and Ireland): **Broadcast Book Services**, Charter House, 29a London Road, Croydon CR0 2RE. Tel: 020 8681 8949. Fax: 020 8688 0615.

- Introduction...................1
1. What is grammar? How should we teach it?....4
2. Implicit and explicit grammar – a small-scale survey..................13
3. 'Bridging the gap' and 'climbing the ladder'.........................20
4. Presenting grammar via authentic texts: receptive skills and recognition 38
5. Productive language, meaningful grammar practice, learner autonomy and peer teaching...................52
6. Grammar in the AS and A2 examinations – preparing, performing and assessing.......................62
- Conclusions 77
- Appendix 1: postgraduate students' difficulties in learning grammar...........79
- Appendix 2: grammar survey 83
- References 86

Introduction

I told someone I was writing a book on teaching grammar to AS and A level students. 'Isn't that a bit late?' he said. 'Does anyone really need such a book?' Well, yes, for a number of reasons. Firstly, because in a foreign language you never stop learning. Also, it was never the case – except in the land of misty nostalgia – that the best O level students, with accurate written foreign language work and all their grammar firmly in place, proceeded on a smooth path through A level to a university language course. Even in those days, sixth form foreign language courses had to build on the grammar learned, deepen knowledge and extend usage. The grammar focus in the preparation for A level courses has shifted over the years. Grammatical accuracy was a principal concern in O level, but following the reforms of 1988, GCSE courses extended skills beyond knowledge of grammar. Pupils were taught how to cope with authentic texts and engage in meaningful communication, but there was a reduced emphasis on accuracy. There has been a further recent shift in focus, with grammar once more occupying a more central role, for example in the National Literacy Strategy, the KS3 pilot and the 2003 GCSE criteria. It may still be the case, however, that GCSE students coming through to an AS course have an uncertain grasp of the grammar of the language studied (see the survey in Chapter 2). They may even have picked up an idea that 'grammar' is necessarily boring and to be avoided if at all possible.

As Eric Hawkins has pointed out:

> *Teachers of languages, both foreign languages and mother tongue, have allowed themselves to be manoeuvred into apologising for mentioning grammar, as a word to be ashamed of. It is not easy to reverse such an attitude.* (Hawkins 1984)

So teachers need to show students starting on their A level language course that grammar can be fun, interesting and very, very useful. Some part of the language learning process must be concerned with gaining an insight into the patterns of language. Teaching grammar is nothing more nor less than using methods which develop insight into such patterns.

The origins of negative views about grammar no doubt lie in the rigid formalism of arid grammar teaching where rules were seen as an end in themselves. Such an approach had its roots in the formal teaching of classical languages. Students might emerge with an intricate knowledge of the uses of the subjunctive but no capacity for stringing words together in a meaningful communication. It was inevitable that the move towards communicative language teaching methods should seek to subordinate grammar to the main goal of communication. Teachers often saw communicative methods as excluding the need for any formal study of structures, unless they were embedded in usable communicative functions. And yet, successful communicative competence must include an element of grammatical competence. How can these equally necessary partners, communicative and grammatical competence, be brought together in the teaching and learning process? The questions become acute at AS/A level.

The first chapter of this book returns to basics to ask a deceptively simple question: What is grammar? Do we all use the word with the same meaning? What is the possible link between grammar in the foreign language class and students' experience of grammar in their English classes? Chapter 2 presents the results of a small-scale survey into grammatical knowledge with students preparing for AS and A2 German exams. Subsequent chapters look at key issues associated with grammar teaching, starting, in Chapter 3, with the practical concerns of bridging the gap between GCSE and A level. Chapter 4 is concerned with the presentation of grammatical items via authentic texts, either printed or from the Internet. Chapter 5 looks at the practice phase of grammar teaching. How can the patterns of language be practised without falling into the deadening routines of meaningless drills? Chapter 6 looks more closely at the area of AS and A2 assessment. The issues raised in each chapter are illuminated and given a practical emphasis by contributions from practising teachers.

The bulk of the book is concerned with grammar as it applies to written and recorded texts, and little space is given to accuracy in oral work. That subject has been very well covered by Anneli McLachlan in another book in this series, *Advancing oral skills* (CILT 2001). Readers interested in the possibilities of learner autonomy discussed in Chapter 5 will also find more on this subject in Barry Jones's book *Developing learning strategies* (CILT 2001).

One aspect of grammar teaching which is not often considered is teachers' own knowledge and understanding of grammar. But it has been clear in recent years that both MFL and English PGCE students may have significant gaps in their knowledge, no doubt as a result of a reduced emphasis on grammar teaching in their school courses. That the problem is not confined to foreign linguists, is shown by Debra Myhill's concerns for grammatical knowledge among her PGCE English students. Her research on *Postgraduate students' difficulties in learning grammar* is included as an appendix and raises issues that are well known to PGCE tutors in foreign languages.

In providing some answers to the questions raised above, the aims of this book may be summarised as follows:

- to consider general issues raised in the debate about teaching grammar;
- to examine the particular problems involved in teaching grammar to AS students entering the sixth form;
- to look at the sequence from teaching receptive grammar for recognition through to productive grammar;
- to discuss how communicative and grammatical competence may be brought together in the teaching and learning process;
- to explore ways of developing independent learning and peer teaching;
- to suggest ideas which show students that grammar can be fun and interesting;
- to consider methods which offer an insight into the patterns of language;
- to examine aspects of assessing grammatical competence in AS/A2 exams.

1

What is grammar?
How should we teach it?

> **Aims** This chapter aims to introduce discussion on:
> - recurrent themes in the debate about grammar teaching;
> - just what we mean by grammar;
> - links to the teaching of English;
> - using the metalanguage of grammar;
> - the role of the mother tongue;
> - current thinking about 'consciousness-raising' and 'form-focused instruction'.

The exemplar should always come first, the precept should always follow, and imitation should be insisted on. (Comenius 1648, quoted by Kelly 1976: 39)

Thus goe forward in every rule:
1. *Reading it over to the children;*
2. *Shewing the plaine meaning in as few words as you can;*
3. *Propounding every piece of it in a short question, following the words of the booke, & answering it yourself out of the words of the book;*
4. *Asking the same questions of them & trying how themselves can answer them, still looking upon their books. Then let them goe in hand with getting it amongst themselves.* (Brinsley 1627, 1648, quoted by Kelly 1976: 50)

Background to the debate

In discussions about the teaching of grammar, there is nothing new under the sun, as the above quotations from the 17th century show. Inductive or deductive, implicit or explicit, rule preceding usage or usage preceding rule, the arguments have swung with the pendulum according to the currently preferred theory and practice. Erasmus 'makes it quite clear to Comenius that he regards rejection of grammar as an excess which was every bit as reprehensible as the opposed devotion to analysis' (Kelly op cit: 37). Krashen's 'natural approach' of the 1980s is an echo of the 'natural method' of Gouin of 1880. The 'cognitive approach' of the 1970s (see Jakobovits 1970) relied on deduction based on rules and thus reminds us of many previous rule-based approaches. In the 1990s, the predominant approach to foreign language teaching has been 'communicative', with a stress on fluency, an emphasis that has tended to push accuracy and grammar teaching to the sidelines.

Johnstone (1994: 9) has pointed out that contemporary attempts to determine the relative merits of the various approaches have been inconclusive:

> *not only because there was no clear superiority in learner performance of one approach over the other, but also because it was not established that teachers in fact used these approaches consistently and exclusively in their teaching. Real teaching was more messy and pragmatic and could not be reduced to one conceptually pure method.*

However, communicative approaches have tended to stress the fun of communicating with the corollary that 'grammar' is necessarily boring and to be avoided if at all possible. Teachers often saw communicative methods as excluding the need for any formal study of structures, unless they were embedded in usable communicative functions. This view has, to some extent, been encouraged by the distribution of marks at GCSE. The exam has quite rightly rewarded the skills of reading and listening, but the weighting of marks allows students to gain high grades with quite limited spoken and written accuracy. Yet successful communicative competence beyond the survival level **must** include an element of grammatical competence, and learning for A level is certainly well beyond survival skills. Even if it were possible to gloss over grammatical concerns to gain a good start in linguistic fluency or to get a good GCSE grade, the demands of courses leading to AS and A2 require clear understanding of patterns heard and read as well as confident and accurate application of grammatical patterns in speaking and writing.

What do we mean by grammar?

We must first seek to define what we understand by grammar. As teachers, we are not concerned with descriptive grammars of the foreign language which seek to set out the whole range of possible uses, rules and exceptions. Nor are we concerned with grammar as logic or training of the mind or any of those higher claims made at various times. Our concern is with pedagogical grammar, that is to say grammar in the context of teaching and learning. For the teacher of foreign languages the grammatical knowledge of students in their mother tongue must be a significant factor and should be (but is rarely) a basis on which to build. Foreign linguists will be glad of valuable new support in the work carried out for the National Literacy Strategy (NLS). McLachlan (2002: 54) has pointed out that, as a result of the NLS in primary schools, pupils will 'arrive with a clearer sense of structure and with more awareness of grammatical structure and grammatical terms.' It may be expected that this awareness will eventually feed through the system to GCSE and to the A level students who are our concern in this book. The website of the National Literacy Strategy, **www.standards.dfes.gov.uk/ literacy** quotes David Crystal, who, when asked to define grammar in terms a nine year-old might understand, suggested: 'Grammar is the study of how we make sentences'. This statement provides a basis for the way grammar is understood in the early years of the NLS. The document continues:

> *It is a very concrete definition, suggesting that sentences are* made *in the same way that a dress or a table might be* made. *A table is made out of wood, put together according to certain conventions, so that it does the job it is intended to do. A sentence is made out of words, put together according to certain conventions, so they do the job they are intended to do [...] Children are taught that a sentence is 'a group of words that go together to make sense'.*

So the view of the NLS is that grammar is composed of building blocks which, when put in place, create meaning. The sentence, as a unit, breaks down into clauses, then into phrases, then into words. Although the ideas suggested here are straightforward, as one would expect for younger pupils, they do imply more advanced notions. For example, naming the building blocks leads to questions of the metalanguage for teaching grammar; understanding the ways in which blocks combine to create meaning implies analysis and cognitive skills, as well as opening the way, where necessary, to concepts of case and inflection. The core of this view, therefore, is that grammar is pattern and structure. Leading on from that is the idea of grammar as rules, to control and order the relationship between pattern and meaning.

The NLS is a recent development, but there have been earlier attempts to focus on grammar in the teaching of mother tongue English. The Kingman report (1988: 3) expressly states that there is no intention 'to plead for a return to old-fashioned grammar teaching and learning by rote'. But the report also rejects:

> *the belief that any notion of correct or incorrect language is an affront to personal liberty [...] Successful communication depends upon a recognition and accurate use of the rules and conventions. Command of these rules and conventions is more likely to increase the freedom of the individual than diminish it.*

The underlying argument here suggests strongly the nature of some of the attacks mounted against formal language teaching in English, and the backwash effects that such arguments might have upon the teacher of foreign languages. The aim of mother tongue teaching, according to Kingman (op cit: 4), is:

> *to enable and encourage every child to use the English language to the fullest effect in speaking, writing, reading and listening [...] It is arguable that such knowledge might be achieved without explicit knowledge of the structure of the language or the ways it is used in society. But there is no positive advantage in such ignorance [...] And since we believe that knowledge about language, made explicit at that moment when the pupil is ready, can underpin and promote mastery as well, the argument is even stronger.*

Surely, most foreign linguists would agree with these sentiments if they were applied to a foreign language rather than English. When both Kingman and Cox (1988) were published, there seemed to be hope of more structured knowledge on which foreign language teachers could build. This author (see Neather 1989) was unduly optimistic! That optimism may now be more fully realised by the National Literacy Strategy.

Metalanguage

The NLS is not shy about using the metalanguage of grammar. Dealing with grammar at word level, the document *Grammatical knowledge for teachers* (NLS website) states: 'Words are classified according to the work they do in a sentence. There are eight word classes', and proceeds to list nouns, verbs and the rest. With regard to the word class 'determiners', the document states, encouragingly for those who are wary of grammatical jargon: 'This classification is very useful because the determiner word class mops up lots of words, which in older grammar hung around on the sidelines.' With regard to the use of appropriate terminology, Kingman is in favour of pupils being given such terminology as a necessary tool:

> *Since [...] teacher and pupil need, in discussion, a word which refers to a class of terms (i.e. pronouns) there is no good reason not to use that term [...] teaching language must involve talking about language, since learning without that activity is slow, inefficient and inequitable in that it favours those whose ability enables them to generalise without tuition.*

The Cox report (1988: 20), which was concerned with the teaching of English mother tongue to pupils aged 5–11, also agreed about some teaching of terminology at that early stage. Support is given for:

> *informed reflection and comments on aspects of language. Words are aids to thinking, tools for learning: they can consolidate implicit awareness. This is a cognitive rationale for using linguistic terms.*

Meta-talk in the secondary school

In the earlier stages of foreign language learning in the secondary school, there are varying views about 'meta-talk', i.e. explicit talk about language and the way it works, using technical linguistic terms. Many teachers feel that using technical terminology adds an unnecessary burden to the load of learning. Myhill (2000: 155) points out that using language to describe language is conceptually challenging. In the A level course one might expect students to be able to handle the formal language of grammar. But there is an argument for allowing students to approach metalanguage via their own formulations. McLachlan (op cit: 55) puts it this way: 'Pupils should be allowed to express rules in their terms, as well as accepting our terms', and she quotes Hawkins (1984: 45) 'The simple principle to be followed throughout is to try to help pupils to conceptualise the *function* of each part of speech before seeking a *name* for it'. Borg (1998:162) suggests small-group meta-talk involving 'meaningful interaction where the content of the conversation is the grammar itself'. Or (Borg op cit) the teacher asks students to look at grammar items in a text and ask questions about differences and similarities, leading the students towards understanding and eliciting as much information as possible in order to formulate conclusions. Borg suggests that there is no need to be dogmatic about metalanguage. Labels may be helpful, but the outcome of meta-talk should not be complex textbook rules.

The role of the mother tongue

So much stress has been laid on the use of the target language in recent years that one almost hesitates to suggest that the mother tongue has a part to play in teaching grammar. Undoubtedly, there are very successful A level teachers who are able to use the target language exclusively including the presentation and discussion of grammar. However, it would seem that part of the cognitive process of understanding how grammar works is to make comparisons. The small-group meta-talk suggested above is most likely to be carried out in English and we should recognise the value of deepening understanding and knowledge by limited forays into comparative linguistics. Cox (1988: 10) suggested that even primary school pupils should be encouraged to:

> *make some systematic comparisons with other languages learned or used in school and in present day British society, so that an interest in linguistic diversity might be encouraged.*

Hawkins, in a chapter entitled 'How language works' (Hawkins 1984: 138), gives a number of examples of discussions, for example about the concept of case, which would need to be carried out by making comparisons to the mother tongue. When giving examples of comparative work relating to English grammar and lexis, Rendall (1998: 48–49) is talking about younger groups of secondary school pupils involved in activities to develop awareness of language, but her points remain equally valid in the context of A level grammar teaching:

> *How can pupils who have not been made explicitly aware of (this characteristic) of the English language know which words to pick from those offered by a bilingual dictionary? […] an essential lesson is being learnt about the nature of the English language: namely, how important it is to thoroughly know any word […] and its function or functions.*

Certainly, an A level discussion about tense usage would be illuminated by comparisons, for example, of the different uses of the perfect and past definite tenses between English and German, or between English and French. Now that Language Colleges are introducing a range of more 'exotic' languages into the curriculum, one must hope that discussion and comparison of grammars will take place in English. It takes an awfully long time to work out only via the target language what is going on grammatically in an agglutinating language like Turkish or a tonal language like Chinese.

Consciousness raising

In asking what we mean by grammar we suggested, following the National Literacy Strategy, that grammar is pattern, and rules relate patterns to meaning. Learning a language must necessarily involve learning and applying rules:

> *[...] whether these rules are consciously formulated by the learners themselves or directly taught [...] whether they are stated in metalinguistic terms or everyday language.* (Mohammed 1995: 49)

Krashen (1985) drew a distinction between unconscious acquisition and the conscious process of learning. In his 'monitor model' of language acquisition, there is no interface between these processes. Consciously learned rules, according to Krashen, are never turned into acquired knowledge. This 'natural acquisition' model has declined in popularity in recent years, partly because 'it rests on the unsupportable distinction between conscious and unconscious knowledge' (Schmidt 1990: 130) and partly because there are many examples around of individuals who learned by formal, 'old-fashioned' methods and have nevertheless achieved a high level of communicative competence. As part of the reaction against Krashen there has been a call, not for a return to old-fashioned formal grammar, but at least to 'consciousness raising'. Consciousness raising was defined by Rutherford (1988: 178) as:

> *a continuum ranging from intensive promotion of conscious awareness through pedagogical rule articulation on the one hand to the mere exposure of the learner to specific grammatical phenomena on the other.*

Schmidt (op cit: 131) sets out 'to assume that both conscious and unconscious processes are involved in second language learning and to assess the contributions of each'. Schmidt makes a useful distinction between **input** (controlled by the teacher) and **intake,** which is 'that part of the input that the leaner notices' (op cit: 139). He agrees that implicit learning is possible, but that its role has been exaggerated and that it 'is best characterised as the gradual accumulation of associations between frequently co-occurring features, rather than unconscious induction of abstract rule systems'. (op cit: 149). Awareness is seen to be essential to successful learning. So, the prerequisite for successful intake is **noticing,** which enables learners to retain forms in the short-term memory. To ensure more permanent retention, forms that have been **noticed** and of which the students have been made aware, need to be **processed.** This is reminiscent of an argument made by Johnson (1988: 89) where he makes a useful comparison between the performance of a skilled language user and a skilled instrumentalist. In both cases, it is not sufficient just to **know about,** it is also essential to **know how.** The sequence is not just 'learn … perform' but 'learn … perform … learn'. The central question is therefore how to supply the feedback that leads to further learning and improvement. Very often, in languages as in music, it is not knowledge which is at fault, but lack of processing ability. An opportunity to process and practice, may be the best way to give feedback, and not explanation.

The issue of awareness and consciousness raising is also central to more recent debates about form-focused instruction (FFI), although FFI goes beyond just grammatical features. Rod Ellis (2001: 1–2) defines FFI as:

> *any planned or incidental instructional activity that is intended to induce the language learner to pay attention to linguistic form. The term form includes phonological, lexical, grammatical and paralinguistic aspects of language.*

Ellis further develops Schmidt's 'noticing hypothesis' and asks in what ways input (positive evidence) can be enhanced to promote noticing, and what kind of feedback (negative evidence) can promote acquisition. He concludes, drawing on other sources, that:

> *attention to form will work most effectively for acquisition if it occurs in the context of meaning-focused communication rather than in instruction that is specifically directed at linguistic forms.*

'Meaning-focused communication' should perhaps be the thread running through this book in its attempt to find answers from practical experience to the question put by Johnstone (1994: 10):

> *How do learners best internalise a system of rules that enables them to be creative and accurate? Is it fundamentally the same process for all learners at all times, or does it vary from individual according to age, aptitude and other factors?*

key points

- There is a need to reassert the place of grammatical accuracy as an equal partner with fluency when teaching A level foreign languages.
- A pedagogical grammar provides students with the patterns which underlie the language and the rules that link patterns to meaning.
- There is a cognitive rationale for using linguistic terminology, but if students have their own concepts of the functions of each part of speech, there is no need to be dogmatic about metalanguage.
- English as mother tongue may play a significant role in raising awareness of grammatical structure by means of comparison and contrast with the foreign language.
- We may aim to raise consciousness about grammar by treating awareness and 'noticing' as prerequisites for successful intake.
- Grammatical structures which have been 'noticed' require process and practice if intake is to be changed into permanent retention.

2

Implicit and explicit grammar – a small-scale survey

Aims	This chapter aims to present the findings of a small-scale survey. Considering the fact that foreign language learners are commonly taught explicit rules of grammar but often fail to apply them when confronted with communicative tasks, the survey seeks to find out: • how well students have learnt the rules; • if students recognise where rules are to be applied; • whether students are better at some rules than others; • how getting the language right is related to explicit rule knowledge.

Chapter 1 raised a number of issues related to grammar teaching. Central to the debate is the extent to which grammar teaching should be explicit or implicit; whether rules should be formulated to aid understanding; whether awareness of a correct grammatical form is possible without being able to formulate a rule. Of particular importance for the first year of the sixth-form course, the AS year, is the question of students' knowledge of grammatical forms and rules on entry to the course, post GCSE. The question of 'bridging the gap' between GCSE and AS will be dealt with specifically in Chapter 3.

In order to illuminate some of the issues concerning implicit and explicit grammar, it was decided to conduct a small-scale survey. The survey involved Year 12 and 13 students studying German. The methodology is based on the study reported in Green and Hecht (1992). Green and Hecht summarise their approach as follows:

Foreign language learners are commonly taught explicit rules of grammar, but often fail to apply them when confronted with communicative tasks. How well have they learnt the rules? Do they recognise where they are to be applied? Are they better at some rules than others? Above all, how is getting the language right related to explicit rule knowledge? (op cit: 168)

To these fundamental questions concerning the relationship between knowledge of grammar and its application we might add questions specific to the English school situation. What is the level of grammatical knowledge in the term immediately following the GCSE exam? What is the evidence of progress in the acquisition of grammatical knowledge between Year 12 and Year 13? With regard to all these questions we must stress at the outset that we are dealing with one institution and a limited number of students. Such a survey cannot have more than a restricted application but it does give a snapshot which is not untypical of a sixth-form or tertiary college whose students enter after a variety of language-learning experiences in a range of school types.

Methodology

Student groups

The test was administered in November 2002 at a tertiary college in the south of England to four groups of students. One group of eleven Year 12 students was preparing to take AS level in June 2003. The second group of seven Year 12 students was preparing for the International Baccalaureate (IB) in 2004. (Students in this college have a choice between AS and IB and make their decision on personal grounds or after taking advice.) Of these IB students, one is Swedish with a very high level of competence in German. One other has a Swiss mother and is near bilingual in English and German.

The third group of seven students in Year 13 also took the test. A further group of two students in Year 13 were native speakers of German and also took the test. They were expected to take A2 in June 2003.

The Test

A list of 20 short sentences was presented to students (see Appendix 2). Each sentence contained an error in basic German grammar involving use of case endings, word order, use of prepositions, etc. All the errors involved grammatical rules which are contained within GCSE grammar lists. The error was underlined in each sentence so that students were not required to hunt for the mistake. Their task was twofold. For each sentence they had to write a corrected version and then state the grammatical rule by which they had made their correction. Corrections were classified under three headings:

(a) Item corrected + rule accurately expressed in technical language.

(b) Item corrected + rule expressed inaccurately or in colloquial terms.

(c) Item corrected but rule given is incorrect or 'N' (no rule) given.

The use of technical language in (a) refers to use of terms such as auxiliary verb, possessive adjective, modal verb, etc. In (b), there was a certain element of subjectivity in deciding whether to accept a student formulation of a rule. For example, is the single word 'feminine' sufficient to indicate knowledge? In general, any indication of knowledge, however brief, was accepted. In category (c), students were able to provide a corrected version of the sentence although no rule (or the wrong rule!) was quoted.

Faulty corrections or omissions were classified under the following categories:

(d) Item incorrect but rule would be correct if properly applied.

(e) Item incorrect + a rule correctly expressed but is not applicable.

(f) Item incorrect and 'N' given for rule, i.e. no answer available.

(g) Item wrongly corrected + wrong rule applied or inadequate explanation.

(h) 'N' + 'N' (no entries in either column).

Categories (d) and (e) are intended to show where rules are known, but cannot be applied correctly (d), or the student tries to apply the wrong rule (e).

Assumptions and expectations

The assumptions underlying this survey may be summarised as follows:

(i) Since the rules in the survey form part of GCSE grammar it might be expected that they form part of the knowledge of Year 12 students.
(ii) If students possess a viable rule, in whatever form they retain it they should be able to produce a corrected version of the faulty sentence.
(iii) Students may be able to arrive at a corrected version even without a rule, because of internalised patterns of repetition in a communicative classroom.
(iv) Year 13 results will show a pattern of progression in learning grammatical rules.
(v) Some rules are more straightforward and easily learned than others.

In addition, it might be assumed that able learners will acquire and apply rules more effectively. Since this survey is anonymous and does not investigate the ability levels of the students, this assumption is not tested.

One further point is that native speakers might be expected to correct all the items, whether or not they can supply rules.

Results

Any item gaining (a), (b) or (c) in the classification explained on p15 is scored as one correct answer.

Year 12 AS students (11 students)

- Individual scores for correct answers ranged from 1 to 8 out of 20.
- No students gave an (a) category answer.
- Total possible correct answers = 11x20 = 220.
- Total of 53 correct answers given = 24% of possible maximum.
- (a) = 0, (b) = 35 = 66% of correct answers, (c) = 18 = 33.9% of correct answers.

Year 12 IB students (7 students)

- Individual scores for correct answers ranged from 3 to 20.
- No students gave an (a) category answer.
- Total possible correct answers = 7x20 = 140.

- Total of 60 correct answers given = 42.8%.
- (a) = 0, (b) = 22 = 36.6%, (c) = 38 = 63.3%.

The score totals for IB students were significantly affected by the only student in the whole survey to score 20 (b=13; c=7), the Swedish student previously mentioned, and a second student (with the Swiss mother) scoring 15 (b=4; c=11). If the IB and AS students are taken together to give a total result for 18 students in Year 12, the totals are as follows:

- Total possible correct answers = 18x20 = 360.
- Total of 113 correct answers given = 31.3%.
- (a) = 0 (b) = 57 = 50% (c) = 56 = 49.5%.

Year 13 A2 students (7 students)

- Individual scores for correct answers ranged from 7 to 12.
- Total possible correct answers = 7x20 = 140.
- Total of 72 correct answers given = 51.4% of possible maximum.
- (a) = 6 = 8.3% of correct answers, (b) = 49 = 68% of correct answers, (c) = 17 = 23.6% of correct answers.

Year 13 native speakers (2 students)

- Student 1 scored 17 correct answers out of 20 items. He omitted three (7, 9 & 17 – see Appendix 2). He gave no rules except for two vague references to word order.
- Student 2 scored 18. One item (item 3) was wrong and one was omitted (12). No rules at all were given.

Conclusions

How does this performance match up to the assumptions and expectations expressed earlier?

(i) **Since the rules in the survey form part of GCSE grammar it might be expected that they form part of the knowledge of Year 12 students.**

Alas, this is clearly not the case. Leaving to one side the two Year 12 IB students who had the best scores in the whole sample, the performance shows significant gaps in knowledge, with no other student in Year 12 scoring more than 8. Seven of the 20 items failed to produce one single corrected version, including supposedly 'elementary' items such as the use of masculine accusative singular and the accusative case after the preposition *über*. Even more worrying for the teacher who must bring this group up to AS level within 8 months is the number of items just left blank.

(ii) **If students possess a viable rule, in whatever form they retain it, they should be able to produce a corrected version of the faulty sentence.**

This assumption is broadly true. There were just 10 examples in the whole survey where students were given (d) for an item, i.e. they stated the rule correctly but failed to provide a correct version of the faulty sentence.

(iii) **Students may be able to arrive at a corrected version even without a rule, because of internalised patterns of repetition in a communicative classroom.**

The results here may be considered surprising. Over the whole sample, 73 out of the total of 185 correct answers (39.4%) were categorised as (c), that is to say the correct answer was given, despite no rule (or the wrong rule) being given. Leaving aside the possibility of a lucky guess, this must indicate that teaching methods up to GCSE may not have laid stress on rule learning (see (i) above) but patterns of grammar have been internalised by repetition. One might also refer the reader to the quotation from Schmidt (1990: 49) given in the previous chapter (p11), who claimed that implicit learning had been exaggerated and that it 'is best characterised as the gradual accumulation of associations between frequently co-occurring features, rather than unconscious induction of abstract rule systems'.

(iv) **Year 13 results will show a pattern of progression in learning grammatical rules.**

Year 13 results show a clear progression in knowledge, if we leave out differences in student ability which are not examined here. Only Year 13 students were able to give answers in category (a), using technical terminology. The range of scores from 7–12 is clearly an improvement and 51.4% of answers given were correct compared with 31.3% for the whole Year 12 sample. In addition, far fewer gaps were left. Nevertheless, there were still three items scoring no corrections (Items 4, 12, 17).

(v) Some rules are more straightforward and easily learned than others.

Conclusions here are hard to draw. The most 'difficult' item for both years was 12, where the present tense was required with *seit*. This is understandable, but who would have predicted that only two students (the IB pair) in Year 12 and two in Year 13 could correct the sentence *er besucht der alte Mann*? One would have assumed that the accusative of masculine nouns was acquired in the first term of the German beginner's course. The items corrected most successfully were the feminine ending on the possessive adjective *meine Freundin* and two items involving the position of the verb in main and subordinate clauses. Fortunately the survey did not arrange the sentences in a pre-selected order of difficulty, as some of these results were not predictable.

Although the two native speakers did not form a significant element of the survey, they confirmed expectations by getting most of the corrections right and by failing to produce any rules.

---

key points

It is important to underline that only very limited conclusions can be drawn from such a small survey. The aim has been to provide a very small piece of evidence for the debates which form the central theme of this book:

- The survey showed an uncertain grasp of grammatical rules in the AS group.
- There was an increased ability to formulate grammatical rules in the A2 group of students.
- It is still possible for a student to correct an error even when he/she cannot formulate an appropriate grammatical rule.
- There is clear evidence that the ability to correct errors is enhanced when a rule can be applied.

3

'Bridging the gap' and 'climbing the ladder'

Aims This chapter aims to introduce discussion on:
- the grammar gap that needs to be bridged between GCSE and AS;
- giving students a new start after GCSE;
- the tools available to assess the level of students' knowledge on entry to the sixth form;
- the techniques for differentiation which will allow all students to move forward;
- making learning (including grammar) fun for the learners;
- developing more sophisticated use of language;
- the possibilities for self-study and getting students to use language independently.

It has become a cliché to speak of 'bridging the gap' between GCSE and the early stages of the AS course. The fact that there is a gap in performance is partly a result of the very wide range of ability among students entering AS level language courses. Some schools and colleges prefer that only students with Grade A or A* at GCSE should be allowed to follow the AS course. However, a college such as Exeter College, described by Martina Esser in the first case study below, takes a range of students including those with Grade C at GCSE. In these entry circumstances it becomes clear immediately that significant work is required to bridge the knowledge gap between Grade C GCSE and a grade at AS. It should be said in passing that the gap between GCSE and AS is also, in part, a result of the system. Since the advent of GCSE in 1988, it has never been the case that reforms in GCSE and A level have been carried through in tandem, so it would be hard to claim that the continuity between the two qualifications is a seamless whole.

In the two case studies below, the experiences and practice of 'bridging the gap' are brought into focus. In the first case study, Martina Esser emphasises a number of crucial points:

- the diagnosis and prognosis of student achievement and performance;
- the importance and the practicalities of differentiation;
- the need to motivate and support students;
- the time available to achieve the aims.

The situation described will be well-known to many teachers but differs from those establishments which have higher barriers to A level course entry and which have the advantage of continuity of teaching between Years 11 and 12.

The second case study also focuses on students entering Year 12 post-GCSE, and the teachers are faced with many similar challenges to the first study. However, the standpoint is different, as in this case the school has a sixth form, and students are able to proceed within the same establishment and have more continuity of teaching. Martin Bowen Jones stresses the importance of motivation in the early stages of the AS course. He also points out the dangers of overloading students in these early stages and the need to maintain a 'fun' element in language studies.

case study 1 | **Dealing with mixed ability in term 1 of AS level German**
by Martina Esser, Head of Modern Languages, Exeter College

Background

Exeter College is a large tertiary College drawing students from a wide range of comprehensive, grammar and independent schools. At the beginning of the academic year 2002–03, 17 students enrolled for AS German.

Observing progress

The department devised a 'tracking sheet' to gain a general overview at the beginning of the academic year and to observe the progression of students from GCSE to A2. This allows the department to make predictions about both progression and how best to help individual students improve their German, with particular regard to bridging the gap between GCSE and AS level German.

There are three key elements to the tracking sheet (see below):

- GCSE points score;
- Initial course-based assessment (ICBA);
- The University of Durham's Advanced Level Information System (ALIS).

The GCSE points score together with the ICBA give a clear picture of an individual's current ability. When this is followed up with the student's ALIS score a picture emerges of the individual's potential.

The GCSE points score for German is calculated from seven subjects: German, English Language, Maths and the four best remaining results. The highest score obtainable under this system – seven A*s (8 points) – is 56. The minimum requirements to start the course are 32 points including grades A–C in German. Since the department began using the tracking sheet we have found a correlation between German A level grades and performance not only in GCSE German but also in English Language and Maths.

The initial course-based assessment (ICBA) is given to all students during their first week. Split into two sections, section one consists of 75 multiple choice questions (1 point each) covering a wide range of GCSE grammar points. In section two students write 100–150 words about themselves, their families and their summer holidays. 25 points are given for range, accuracy and content. An overall grade is given as a percentage.

The third factor in the department's tracking sheet – the University of Durham's Advanced Level Information System (ALIS) is used to provide target grades for students. Target grades are derived from a predicted UCAS points score based on a student's average incoming GCSE score. For our purposes, the UCAS points are changed into grade predictions on the tracking sheet. We use these predictions for target setting with each individual student and students who are predicted with U are told their prediction is E so as not to demotivate them.

2002 German AS tracking sheet

students

	Former school	GCSE Points Score	GCSE German	GCSE Eng Lang	GCSE Maths	ICBA	ALIS to be added	AS	A2	Comments
A	Independent	N/A	not taken	B	E	32%	U/N			late starter bad attendance
B	Comprehensive	33	C	C	E	34%	U/N			
C	Comprehensive	35	B	B	B	39%	D			
D	Comprehensive	33	C	D	D	49%	U/N			
E	Comprehensive	38	A	D	D	44%	E/D			
F	Grammar	38	C	C	C	44%	E/D			student left after a few weeks
G	Comprehensive	39	A	A	D	39%	E			
H	Comprehensive	47	A	B	A	74%	C/B			
I	Comprehensive	40	B	A	D	34%	E/D			
J	FE College	39	C	D	D	49%	No data			Finnish
K	Comprehensive	37	B	B	C	50%	D/C			
L	Comprehensive	35	B	C	C	40%	U			late starter
M	Independent	43	A	B	B	53%	D			
N	Comprehensive	51	A*	A	A	67%	C/B			
O	Comprehensive	49	A	B	A	64%	C/B			
P	Comprehensive	43	C	B	B	42%	D/C			
Q	Comprehensive	52	A*	A*	B	56%	B			

Advanced Pathfinder 5: *Getting to grips with grammar* – 23

A further aspect the department considers is the 'value added' aspect of a score. 'Value added' is the term used when students get better grades than predicted, and is calculated by comparing the actual UCAS points the students achieve with their prediction. Thus a student who gets a B grade at AS level (50 UCAS points) and who was predicted a C grade (40 UCAS points) has a positive value-added score in that subject. 'Value-added' is a relative measure, dependent on the ability of the students. If your intake of students is very bright it will be no surprise that they all leave with A–C grades. But if the students are less able, then in value-added terms their achievement will be equally good, or better, if they leave with C–E grades. The positive aspects of this system are that it allows the college to give students realistic targets in their AS and A levels based on their ability.

By averaging out all the positive and negative scores for a subject, we can see whether a subject as a whole has added value to the students or not. In the academic year 2001–2 our MFL department did particularly well, with German, Spanish and French topping the College tables for both AS and A2 level.

Target setting for the 17 AS group students

As can be seen from the tracking sheet above, the 2002 AS group consisted mostly of students of moderate to low ability, especially with reference to their linguistic skills. A fair number of the lower ability students had a combination of low GCSE scores, low ICBA scores (less than 50%), and low ALIS predictions at AS level.

The realistic targets set for this group were to ensure that:

- students B, D, G and L passed at grade E;
- all other students passed at least at their target grades predicted by ALIS.

Achieving the targets set

To achieve the above aims differentiation by task was essential so that weaker students could close gaps in their knowledge of grammar and so that students who knew their GCSE grammar did not wait while other students caught up. Bridging units usually occupy one term, but with the 2002 group differentiation continued in terms 2 and 3.

Students also received individual learning support for one hour per week over 10 weeks. Learning support is offered to students in danger of failing the course. A combination of low GCSE points scores, GCSE grades B or C in German, ICBA results below 50% and low ALIS predictions justify such a step even during the bridging period. We have found individual support for the weakest students invaluable in building up confidence.

How to close the gap

This section focuses mainly on the teaching of grammar, although the Exeter College course also includes strategies for developing lexis and study skills which are not dealt with here.

Our four bridging topics are similar to some GCSE topics, but cover the issues raised in more depth: families; food and drink; holidays and tourism; and important issues for young people. Units covered in term 1 are shorter than subsequent units, to give a sense of achievement and to review basic grammar.

At Exeter College we take the view that grammar needs to be covered from scratch, as it cannot be taken for granted that each student has the same knowledge and understanding. Taking time over the basics is time well spent. In-depth explanations on the board are followed by class work and group work to reinforce points, and grammar drills are used for homework.

Vocabulary lists and grammar drills always arise from reading and listening texts which cover a specific topic, and soon lead to micro writing and then to writing whole paragraphs and eventually short essays as required for the AS exams. As soon as micro-writing within a particular topic is possible, differentiation by outcome is the basis for any grades given at such an early stage.

During the bridging period grades are awarded according to effort and improvement on the previous performance. Stronger candidates are always invited to write more than the bare minimum. Weaker candidates are advised to stick to short, straightforward structures and to concentrate on getting right the grammatical areas which have been covered. Mistakes outside these areas are not pointed out in their work so as not to discourage weaker students.

Students are always encouraged to use both language and ideas from reading and listening texts. While the idea of 'copying' parts of sentences from another text is often questioned by students at first, learning to manipulate language by changing the word-order or substituting words with synonyms is valuable practice and provides a safety net for students who don't know what to write.

Differentiation in the sixth form

Differentiation is an important part of the bridging period but could well continue throughout the AS and A2 course. Realistically speaking, we have as many different abilities sitting in front of us as we have students in the classroom and we have to find a way to deal with this.

As described above, the 2002 AS level group was of mixed ability. Therefore we used the information gathered about our students not only to identify where learning support was needed for the weakest, but also to organise the class into four ability groups. Introduced by the end of September, the groups were reconsidered every six to eight weeks to allow for the progress that some weaker students made, and to support students who came with higher GCSE grades but were now beginning to feel the strain. The emphasis was to keep everybody motivated and enjoying the course.

The department currently operates four sessions per week for AS, adding up to 4 hours 50 minutes. Some of these sessions are used for open-access work and differentiation. These sessions are usually set up to consolidate grammar and content and can take different shapes:

a) students work within their ability groups
b) stronger students work with weaker peers
c) students are allowed to choose their group according to the task and activity they want to do.

Most of these differentiation sessions in groups revolve around four different activities which last between 15 and 25 minutes each. For example:

1. Listening activity;
2. Speaking activity or short Writing activity;
3. Reading activity;
4. Grammar activity or Vocabulary acquisition.

Listening and reading activities

Listening and reading activities are differentiated:

- by text (easier text for weaker students);
- by task (the same text, but easier exercises);
- by providing extra help.

Speaking activities

These can either be led by the foreign language assistant or by the teacher and may cover either the topic content or reinforce a particular grammar point.

Writing activities

Writing activities should be very short and focused. By way of differentiation the strongest students could be asked to write a paragraph on a particular topic covered recently in class. An easier option would be to write bullet points on the same topic and for the weakest students a skeleton text could be provided, which they finish by themselves or with the help of their whole group.

If a lesson does not lend itself to the carousel set-up described above, part of the session, normally the reinforcement part, could be managed by self-access. Here texts or grammar exercises are offered in two or even three different versions. Students can take responsibility for their own learning which is very important in the sixth form. They choose their task and feel encouraged by their successes to try out more difficult versions. Self-access must be the ultimate form of differentiation, but we have found that to be able to do it well a great deal of time and dedication and a good bank of resources are needed to set it up.

Grammar can be differentiated too. Checking through exercises in grammar books identifies which group within our class they may serve best. To practise a particular grammar point we ask students:

1. to recognise and underline points in a short text, e.g. modal verbs;
2. to fill in gapped sentences or texts – differentiated by offering the answers jumbled up if needed;
3. to practise drills, which are in themselves differentiated by the lexis used;
4. to produce short sentences which contain the grammar point covered;
5. to produce a short paragraph.

If there is no time to produce such a range of exercises from scratch, exercises from old GCSE books and a range of Grammar books are provided for students to choose from.

However, the principle that recognition comes before production is important and some students will need to work through several recognition exercises and easier drills before they can begin to tackle production. As part of a self-access session or a session with 'set' groups, this works well, as students will be working at their own pace and their own ability.

Conclusions to case study 1

The situation described in this case study is characterised by the wide range of abilities within the group and also by the relatively limited teaching time available for teachers to cover all the necessary ground. The department's answer to this is a highly organised system of diagnosis on arrival, working towards clear targets, motivation and encouragement of individual students and differentiation by task and by group. Not all the points made will be relevant to every situation, but there are underlying principles which all teachers of AS level should find applicable:

- have a clear understanding of the starting point for each student;
- set realistic targets for the student;
- provide individual support where needed;
- explore ways to differentiate teaching input and set tasks so that both are appropriate to each student's level of knowledge.

---

case study 2 | **Avoiding student drop-out: a pain-free, fun-filled introductory unit**
by Martin Bowen Jones, Head of Languages, Llanishen HS, Cardiff and Advisory Teacher for MFL, Cardiff LEA

My experience as Advisory Teacher has shown me that the introduction of the new AS exam – with its daunting list of grammar to be covered – has led many schools to dispense with their old bridging units and 'dive straight in', with an initial concentration on 'remedial' grammar work to 'bring them up to scratch'.

I would argue that such an approach can be damaging to many students, especially those for whom the AS exam was designed, namely the students who have chosen a language as their 'fourth' subject, or those who are not perhaps sufficiently able to cope with the full A level. Languages already have a problem attracting large numbers at post-16 level, and yet this approach puts off many who have enjoyed languages at GCSE level. The Nuffield Languages Inquiry report (2000: 51) noted that,

> *Many students, even those with the highest GCSE grades, drop out within a few weeks of starting an A level language course because they find it too difficult.*

A well written article in the TES (Reed 2001) commented that,

> *weaker pupils [...] are increasingly overwhelmed by the speed and amount of new structures and skills demanded of them. [They] are too soon being fed a diet of exam-oriented material. [...] Year 12 students are being denied the time to mature into the skills required.*

I am convinced that it is a grave mistake to 'go in at the deep end' in this way. This only serves to make students feel that they are hopelessly unprepared for the new course, with the emphasis on what they don't know or are no good at. Their confidence and motivation can be seriously undermined at a vital time, when their enthusiasm should be at its greatest.

Some ideas to bridge the gap

Creating the right atmosphere

An extract from the Cardiff LEA draft policy on learning and teaching sums up for me what our first few weeks should try to achieve:

> *A state of relaxed alertness is conducive to effective learning [...] effective teaching creates a stimulating environment and an atmosphere where learners feel secure.*

This state of relaxed alertness can be achieved in a number of ways. Whereas many of my colleagues do this through food and drink (tea and coffee to keep students alert, biscuits to help them relax), I favour a style of teaching that moves away from the demands of the syllabus and allows pupils to play around with language for a while, and feel comfortable doing so, in a way that GCSE rarely allowed.

Building on prior knowledge

My first lesson with the AS class is always: 'The day I got my results' (see p36). This allows students to revisit the language of daily routine, but careful questioning can elicit fairly detailed, extended responses that can go way beyond the limitations of GCSE. There is great scope for brainstorming adjectives and emotions, and using dictionaries to broaden the list to include 'delighted, thrilled, relieved, disappointed, petrified, proud, shocked, annoyed', etc. Using a writing frame, students have to produce a piece of narrative and descriptive writing that includes a full account of how they reacted, what their results were, how they celebrated, their parents' and friends' reactions, etc, while they also have to state what they have chosen for AS level and why, and why they gave up certain subjects. This lesson always produces a great deal of fairly excited chat, with pupils prompting and challenging each other. The written outcomes are invaluable as a guide to the range of abilities in the new set.

Promoting spontaneity

At GCSE students are rarely expected to speak in situations that are not carefully structured, well rehearsed or teacher-led. We cannot, therefore, expect them to be able to take part in lively discussions or arguments on the AS topics without developing their ability to talk spontaneously. I find the most effective way to do this is through games and jokes. Here are some examples.

Definitions

Divide the class into two teams. Issue students with a series of cards with individual words on them. These can be simple nouns, place names or people. Students have to give clues as to the word. Start with easy words like 'Scotland' or 'cricket', and students very quickly have to think on their feet and improvise linguistically. This is best played against the clock.

Who's in the bag?

Students have a bag containing cards bearing the names of actors, politicians, cartoon characters, sport stars, etc. It is played in the same way as the above game but needs more guidance from the teacher, such as the phrase 'The singer who sang [...] The actor who was in [...]' – a great way of practising relative pronouns.

Whole-class gap filling

Gap filling is a significant feature of the new AS and A2 exams. My approach is to make this a whole-class activity using jokes as short texts, with pupils required to call out possible solutions. This can be done with the OHP, but is very effective using PowerPoint, when each sentence – and the correct answer – can be revealed at the click of a mouse. Here are some examples, which work well because they are on the familiar GCSE themes of school, parts of the body and films.

Complétez les blagues: scènes de classe

Dans une classe de terminale, un prof de sciences naturelles est en train de donner un cours sur la circulation du ☐☐☐☐.

Voulant donner un exemple pratique, il dit aux élèves:
– *Vous voyez, si je fais le trépied ou si je marche sur les mains pendant un certain temps, le* ☐☐☐☐ *va s'accumuler dans ma tête, et j'aurai le* ☐☐☐☐☐☐ *tout rouge. Vous êtes d'accord?*

– Oui (en chœur).

– *Maintenant, pouvez-vous m'expliquer pourquoi lorsque je suis en position debout, le* ☐☐☐☐ *ne s'accumule pas pour autant dans mes* ☐☐☐☐☐.

Et là un des élèves répond:
– *C'est parce que vos* ☐☐☐☐☐ *ne sont pas* ☐☐☐☐☐.

Answers: *sang | sang | visage | sang | pieds | pieds | vides*

Un instituteur fait remarque à un de ses élèves:
– C'est très curieux mais, sur ce devoir de mathématiques, il me semble reconnaître l'écriture de ton père.

– Ça, répond le gamin, ce n'est pas étonnant: je ☐☐ ☐☐☐☐ ☐☐☐☐☐ ☐☐ ☐☐☐ ☐☐☐☐☐.

Answer: *je me suis servi de son stylo.*

Source: www.misterblague.com

> ### Complétez les blagues: le monde selon le cinéma
>
> ☐☐ ☐☐☐☐ ☐☐☐☐☐☐ est visible de n'importe quelle fenêtre parisienne.
>
> Toute scène dans Londres se passe à proximité de ☐☐☐ ☐☐☐.
>
> Tout personnage survit facilement à des scènes de guerre. Sauf s'il montre à quelqu'un la photo de ☐☐ ☐☐☐☐☐ et de ses ☐☐☐☐☐☐☐, ce qui garantit ☐☐ ☐☐☐☐ ☐☐☐☐☐☐☐☐☐.
>
> Answers: *la Tour Eiffel | Big Ben | sa femme | enfants | sa mort prochaine*

Source: www.courtois.cc/ordicinema.htm

Such short reading texts are enjoyable and motivating, and come as a breath of fresh air to most students after the tedium of exam-orientated work in Year 11. They are easily obtained from the internet using a search engine. Some amusing texts worth searching for and adapting in this way include:

- *Les lois de Murphy;*
- *Les punitions de Bart Simpson;*
- *Ce qu'elle veut vraiment dire;*
- *Le jeu de «C'est bien – C'est mal – C'est pire»;*
- *Quelques mauvaises approches pour draguer;*
- *Six semaines, six mois, six ans.*

Board game

This is a variation on the game 'Just a minute' without the interruptions. Students simply talk unscripted for 30 seconds on the subject they land on.

Ce que je vais faire quand je quitte l'école	Ma famille	Mon sport préféré	Les frites
La musique que j'écoute le matin			Quelqu'un que je n'aime pas
Ce que j'ai regardé à la télé hier			Le week-end dernier
Un week-end parfait			Paris
Pourquoi j'aime mon école			Noël
Mes vacances idéales			Mon prof préféré
Mon film préféré	Les matières que j'ai choisies	Le petit déjeuner	Dimanche

Extended reading

After GCSE, students are unfamiliar with tackling longer, denser reading passages with significant amounts of new vocabulary. Texts like those above are a gentle introduction, but students do need to develop advanced reading skills fairly quickly. An ideal text is, in my opinion, one that focuses on students' approaches to learning, and promotes discussion of language-learning techniques. This is an aspect that is strongly advocated in the QCA schemes of work for KS3, and is highly relevant at AS level because of the need to address the key skill of improving learning and performance. A good example of such a text is *Comment travailler à la maison quand on est au lycée* – it is accessible, full of cognates, and full of sound advice for students (see **www.cyberprofs. net/conseil_lycee_maison.asp**).

Creative writing

The second piece of extended writing I give my students is based on a picture stimulus. Any photo can lead to some imaginative suggestions as to the situation, with students required to invent some biographical details, give a brief character portrait and a description of the setting. Ideally, however, the picture used should offer scope to go beyond mere description and hint at themes and topics that are more typically AS/A level. The example here has the potential to throw up a wealth of more 'mature' vocabulary, with students bringing up the issues of war and peace, love, protest, rebellion, freedom, danger, courage. Such an activity means that it is the students themselves who start to bridge the gap, building on their prior knowledge to extend their range of language.

© 2001, Barbara Ludman/iwitness

Teaching grammar

For most teachers grammar is the major concern about making the step up to A level. Teachers may be sceptical of the value of some of my approaches and feel there is no time for the sort of activities outlined, preferring instead to press on with grammar from the outset. I feel that an over-emphasis on grammar in the first few weeks can be counter-productive.

However, it must be pointed out that many of the activities above provide opportunities to deal with key grammar points, although I advocate as a starting point the following exercise that my students have found challenging but good fun – as it puts them on a 'level playing field', and at the same time encourages lively debate about the nature of sentence structure and parts of speech.

The following sentences are in an invented language. Isolate the individual words and work out their meanings.

a)	amóndriistéekó	A woman is there.
b)	izgétuistéimpírno	The dog is ill.
c)	istéimpirnoizóndri?	Is the woman ill?
d)	amgétuistéimpírno	A dog is ill.
e)	izgétuistéekó	The dog is there.
f)	amgétuistéekó	A dog is there.
g)	amóndriistéimpírno	A woman is ill.
h)	izóndriistéekó	The woman is there.

What is the word for: woman?
dog?
ill?
there?
a?
the?
is?

My students have been thrilled to be told that the source of this exercise is an old Oxford Entrance paper.

I believe strongly that teachers need to give their classes activities of this kind as a warm-up before addressing the demands of the syllabus, both to create the right atmosphere and to build up their confidence. Just because they are having fun doesn't mean they are not learning!

Le jour où j'ai reçu mes résultats *(guided composition)*

Je n'oublierai jamais ce jour-là. Je ... Tu as bien dormi? Tu t'es levé(e) à quelle heure? Tu pouvais manger?	**Le soir ...** Qu'est-ce que tu as fait? Avec qui? Tu t'es bien amusé(e)?
Quand je suis arrivé(e) à l'école, ... Qui as-tu vu? Qu'est-ce que tu as dit/pensé?	**J'avais déjà décidé d'étudier le français, parce que ... C'est une matière que j'aime beaucoup, parce que ... Pour améliorer mon français, je dois ...**
Je me sentais ..., parce que ...	
Après avoir reçu mes résultats, je ... Qu'est-ce que tu as fait? Comment as-tu réagi? Et tes copains/copines? Avec qui as-tu parlé?	**Quant à l'avenir, quand j'aurai fini mes A levels, j'espère ...** Pourquoi as-tu choisi le français? Comment feras-tu des progrès en français? Que feras-tu dans l'avenir?
Mes parents étaient ... Comment ont-ils réagi? Qu'est-ce qu'ils t'ont dit? Et tes grands-parents, etc?	

Conclusions to case study 2

The second case study focuses, above all, on the need to offer support to students entering upon their AS language course. The emphasis here is on taking care not to switch off initial enthusiasm by too abrupt a plunge into 'remedial' grammar. Students at this stage need to be motivated and to have their confidence boosted. Essential skills are certainly not neglected, but the teaching aims to create a relaxed atmosphere, link in to prior knowledge and to offer a sense of fun and enjoyment.

key points
- There is a need for initial diagnosis of students' language knowledge and projection of their likely progression, especially where they have changed institutions.
- Differentiation by task allows students to work at their own level of performance.
- It is important that recognition of grammatical features precedes production.
- There is a danger of overloading students on entry to the AS course.
- It is important to maintain a 'fun' element for the sake of students' confidence and motivation.
- Work on developing extended reading skills and creative writing.

4

Presenting grammar via authentic texts: receptive skills and recognition

| **Aims** | This chapter aims to introduce discussion on:
• authenticity and types of text;
• current course-book approaches to topics and texts;
• receptive grammar and recognition skills;
• promoting 'noticing' and awareness;
• authentic texts and the Internet. |
|---|---|

Authenticity

The term authenticity is widely used and may be taken to refer either to text or task. A straightforward definition of authenticity of text might be that the text was originally written for a native speaker of the language and has not been edited in any way. This is a long way from earlier texts that were concocted especially for teaching a particular point of grammar. The current view of authenticity inevitably raises problems for the teacher and the student. It necessarily means that a given text may contain a wide variety of structures and lexis, and that such texts are difficult to set into a linear sequence of language learning. Students are therefore encouraged to drop the idea that they need to understand every word and phrase and learn how to develop reading skills which skim such an authentic document for the information they need.

Because of the range and variety of language in truly authentic texts, textbook writers (and also examination setters) may back away from the pure version of authenticity and edit texts, even if only marginally, to exclude items perceived as difficult, or to shorten the original.

A second element of authenticity lies in the appearance and presentation of the text. So students are used to the idea that the text before them, in the coursebook or on the exam paper, at least resembles an original newspaper article. One might express some reservations about the meanings taken on by the word 'authentic'. At a more philosophical level, it may even be queried whether the experience of reading an apparently authentic article during a school period or a test can ever be truly authentic, in that the context of reading is wholly different from the original intention of the writer. Widdowson made this distinction as early as 1978, when he drew a distinction between 'genuineness' and 'authenticity'.

> *Genuineness is a characteristic of the passage itself and is an absolute quality. Authenticity is a characteristic of the relationship between the passage and the reader and has to do with appropriate response.*

There is also a sense in which the debate about authenticity has so concentrated on newspaper and magazine articles and presentation, that one even finds it necessary to argue whether a literary text can be reckoned to be 'authentic'.

(Parts of the above section are adapted from Neather (2001, pp26–27.)

A level coursebooks

Compared with the paucity of provision in earlier times, teachers now have an embarrassment of choice when selecting an A level coursebook, at least in French, German and Spanish. There are obviously differences of style, presentation and content in the range of coursebooks on offer. But the centralised criteria for the A level examinations and the general agreement as to the current state of the art in language teaching mean that coursebooks do have certain characteristics in common. One might summarise these characteristics as follows:

(i) Chapters (also called Units) are organised around the range of topics forming the content of A level syllabus specifications. The problem for authors and publishers is that the choice of topics varies between the Exam Boards. So this is an area where there may be differences between books. Some publishers actually have an agreement with a Board to recommend their book, although such agreements do not make a book exclusive to one Board.

(ii) Topics are one organising principle of the books, but all present the student with an initial grid setting out, for each chapter, the topics, grammar focus, communicative functions, lexis and skills development.

(iii) The topic content is presented through the medium of authentic text extracts drawn from a variety of sources, but mainly current journals and newspapers.

(iv) Presentation and page layout are lively, varied, copiously illustrated and often in colour. The effort to present a lively page layout sometimes leads to a rather 'busy' page presentation which might become wearisome and does not always make it easy for the student to follow a sequence.

(v) Books may be in a single volume or two volumes (depending on whether a decision has been taken to split the AS and A2 parts of the course). All courses now appear as a package, containing student's book, teacher's resource book and recorded material. In addition there may be a student workbook and further resources in the shape of CDs or video.

(vi) All books present a summary of grammar as a reference for students.

(vii) All books contain assessment materials. Some offer assessment packs geared up to separate board requirements.

Teaching grammar from authentic texts

From point (ii) above, we note that authors do signpost a line of grammatical progression through coursebooks, despite the problems indicated earlier in providing a grammar focus within the flood of material present in any authentic text. From the teacher's point of view, therefore, the question is how best to present and practice that grammar focus.

A first point is to make a distinction between **receptive** and **productive** grammar. It is perfectly possible to build up a reading knowledge of a language, where key grammatical points such as inflexions and tense usage are recognised, even though the reader would not have the skills to speak or write the foreign language using those grammatical forms productively. The same point is made by Martina Esser in her case study in Chapter 3 (p25) when she states, 'the principle that recognition comes before production is important and some students will need to work through several recognition exercises and easier drills before they can begin to tackle production'. It must be stressed that the receptive skills of recognition and recall are certainly not 'passive', as such skills were once described. Belyaev (1963) followed Piaget and Lado in stressing that the learner is always active in comprehending the input because active mental processes are involved in recognition and comprehension. To return to the discussion in Chapter 1, (pp10–11) we may say that reception and recognition involve 'noticing' and input, but do not proceed to intake, which requires processing and production. Johnstone (1994: 12) offers the following summary with reference to speaking and listening, but the points he makes are equally applicable to reading and writing:

> *Grammar for comprehension then is likely to differ from grammar for production in two ways. First, it will probably be more wide-ranging and developed; second, it will require careful attention on the part of the listener since it will be a basis on which the listener will work out what the speaker means. It will make sense then for learners from an early point to be taught a wide range of grammar for comprehension, even though much of this may not be used in production for a considerable time. It will make less sense for their grammar to be limited to that which they need for their own production – yet this is precisely the assumption on which at present many course materials are based.*

We shall be concerned here with recognition of grammatical features in written texts. Following Nuttall (1982) and L'Huilier et al. (2000), we shall first consider cohesive devices and discourse markers and then move on to verb tenses and sentence syntax. L'Huilier et al. (op cit: 17) define text cohesion as:

> *the explicit process whereby sentences or utterances are linked together to form a text. Cohesive devices (ties) are therefore those words or phrases which enable the writer/speaker to establish relationships across sentence or utterance boundaries and which help to link the different parts of the text together.*

Nuttall (op cit: 83) points out that these ties 'are so straightforward that their potential difficulty is overlooked […] the reader who does not know what a pronoun refers to […] will not be able to establish its signification.'

The examples given here are from French and German, but similar or parallel examples could be devised from any language. Although the grammatical markers may vary between languages, cohesion is a necessary characteristic of all texts which aim to convey meaning.

Examples of grammatical cohesion

Personal pronouns

Whether in their subject or object form:

- **Un homme** est entré. **Il** s'est dirigé vers le bar.
- **Werner** ist zu mir gekommen. Ich habe **ihm** gesagt, er ...

In each case, the pronouns point backwards to the preceding noun, and cannot be understood without that cohesive relationship.

Demonstratives and definite articles

- Regarde **ce** tableau. **Il** est magnifique.
- Er kaufte **den** Wagen nicht, weil ihm **der hier** besser gefiel.

Possessives

Like definite articles and demonstratives, possessives belong to the class of specific determiners:

- La robe de Martine est blanche. **La mienne** est rouge.
- Helgas Kleid ist weiß. **Meines** ist rot.

The above examples show determiners referring **back** to a previously mentioned referent; (a process known technically as anaphora). It is also possible to refer **forward** (cataphora).

- Par **sa** voix on reconnaît déjà Michel de loin.

Comparatives

In the case of comparative statements, the relationship within a text is not one of co-reference but of contrast:

- Il travaille **mieux que** son frère.
- Er arbeitet **so fleißig, wie** ich.

42 – Advanced Pathfinder 5: *Getting to grips with grammar*

Connectors

Conjunctions, adverbs or adverb phrases are used to establish connections of space or time between different parts of a text.

- *Voilà notre maison. **En haut** vous trouverez la salle de bains. **En bas**, c'est le salon.*
- ***Zuerst** machen wir Pause, **dann** gehen wir weiter.*

Punctuation

Although not technically part of grammar, punctuation has a significant effect on understanding the way in which a text functions.

Discourse markers

Words such as 'however', 'although', 'furthermore', 'namely' are not, of course, grammatical structures but they are key elements in signalling meaning to a reader. A little word like *mais* or *doch* may provide an explanation which unlocks the problem of more complex structures.

Verbs and tense cohesion

Recognition of tense and aspect is an essential element in receptive grammar. For example, the interplay of tenses in the French example below or the change to the historic present in the German narrative:

- *L'ordinateur **a remporté** un grand succès. Il **est** présent dans une maison sur trois. Il y a trois ans ils **n'étaient** que 400 000 connectés à l'Internet.*
- *Seine Fußspitzen **fassten** Gestein. Er **hockte** in der Nische. Sein Herz **klopfte** zum Zerspringen ... Der Zug **kriecht** heran, langsam wie immer an dieser Stelle. Rolf **sitzt** sprungbereit in der Nische.*

In addition to the connectors and markers indicated above, recognition of markers, e.g. for plurals, is important and case inflection is a major part of receptive grammar in languages such as German or Russian.

Tasks for recognising the grammar of texts

Students should be encouraged to work with the cohesive grammar of texts by doing tasks which require recognition, for example:

- underline or highlight connectors, discourse markers and specific referents such as personal pronouns and demonstratives;
- indicate the links between a pronoun and its referent;
- focus on plural markers or case endings to establish links between words;
- replace punctuation in a section of text where it has been removed;
- reassemble a text that has been cut up;
- match halves of sentences selected from the text and jumbled up;
- work with a gapped text and fill the gaps by drawing from a list of items.

There is certainly nothing new about these suggestions. Some of these tasks (e.g. matching halves of sentences) form part of the standard fare for target language tests in exams. All of them are seen as developing reading skills. The point to emphasise here is that they also form part of the process of raising awareness of **grammar** and offer a significant and important phase of **recognition.** All the suggestions above relate to written texts, but a parallel series of tasks can be devised for listening texts:

- deduce the meaning of unfamiliar words;
- infer information not explicitly stated;
- recognise indicators for introducing an idea, changing topic, emphasis, clarification, expressing a contrary view;
- predict subsequent parts of the text;
- identify discourse markers in the text that can help to recognise a pattern of organisation.

(See also Neather (2001: 60–61).)

Authentic texts and the Internet

The range of available authentic texts has been immeasurably increased by all that is now available on the Internet. Even the best coursebooks become dated and hours spent scanning newspapers and journals may only yield a very few nuggets. But the Internet allows teachers to search very specifically for particular topics and key words. There is no doubt that this resource has become essential for all teachers of foreign languages, especially those teaching in years 12 and 13. But the sheer volume of material presents its own problems. And when a good text has been located, how should it be used to the best advantage? There are general principles of methodology with which teachers will approach any authentic text, but the particular issues raised by the use of Internet texts for teaching grammar are explored in the following case study.

case study 3 | Using the Internet to present grammar
by Sabine Gläsmann, Lecturer at the School of Education, University of Sheffield

Why read texts on-line?

Presenting students with continually new and up-to-date authentic materials is one of the major challenges every language teacher faces. At various points in the exam, for example during oral examinations, students are expected to display their knowledge of current affairs in the country of the target language, yet few schools are fortunate enough to have access to satellite news programmes or a subscription to a major newspaper.

Over recent years, the Internet has more and more become the primary source for authentic materials. Considering that newspapers, television channels, discussion groups and an immense number of organisations have created a presence for themselves on-line, there is now no easier or cheaper way to keep students and staff up-to-date with current affairs. Printed texts may quickly become dated but the Internet is updated constantly. Whereas scouring a newspaper for topical items can take a considerable time, searching the Internet presents the user with a host of appropriate materials in a matter of seconds. Furthermore, being able to use the Internet properly is a considerable skill in the employment market, and allowing students to practise this skill in the foreign language classroom leads to an increased knowledge not only of grammar and lexis, but also of ICT skills. Students are usually well versed in the art of 'surfing the Web'. Harnessing the motivation they will bring to working on-line for language learning purposes may well lead to a more independent learning approach.

Grammar? What grammar?

Authentic texts on the Internet are similar to those in printed format in that they are rarely specifically related to a particular grammar point. So the teacher needs to search the Web carefully for material suitable for a particular class. When looking for material, two starting points can be taken as selection criteria:

(i) the teacher already has a grammar point in mind and is searching the Internet for a text which may be used to teach this specific grammar point; or

(ii) whenever the teacher comes across a text which may be suitable for teaching a certain grammar point, this text gets entered into a database, slowly building up a library of materials for future use.

In reality, a combination of these two approaches is likely. Initially, material will be sought to cover certain grammatical aspects but this search will reveal further texts which the teacher will put to one side to be used when appropriate. By creating a folder for Web-related materials in the department, it is possible to share good practice and avoid duplication of work.

Working with the text

Topic or grammar

When it comes to choosing a text, some will be more suitable for presenting grammar than others, but few are likely to stress a grammatical point just so it can be covered successfully in a foreign language classroom. Some grammatical points, such as imperatives, will be found on 'hints and tips' pages, be it on women's magazines pages giving tips for a healthier lifestyle, or on a mountain rescue site giving advice on safe walking. Similarly, most newspaper reports will be written in a past tense, whereas wish lists for Christmas will make use of the conditional. Frequently, however, the grammar point in question may appear only a few times and teachers should be aware of the cost/benefit ratio related to using a text which might cover a grammar point more deliberately, yet is completely unrelated to any topic currently being covered. Any authentic text will present the class with a flood of new vocabulary, which will need to be addressed before the grammar in question can be tackled. It might therefore be more beneficial to find texts related to the current topic and use such texts to illustrate and present grammar in an authentic context, rather than teaching it from scratch.

Solving vocabulary problems – using pop-up boxes

When vocabulary needs to be covered in conjunction with grammar, it is, for example, possible to create a Word document which mirrors the text on the website, but which will supply the students with pop-up boxes of vocabulary should they need this aid. To do this, the word in question should be highlighted. By going to 'Insert' on the menu bar and choosing 'Comment', a translation can be typed in which will 'pop up' if the student moves the mouse over the highlighted word in question (see below). This feature was originally developed to supply comments for memos, but it works just as well in the languages classroom – whether it is used to explain vocabulary, phrases, or, indeed, grammatical structures. It is, for example, possible to prepare a text by highlighting the grammar point in question throughout a text and giving explanations in the 'Comment' box – or, indeed, to ask students to do so for homework, submitting the piece of work on a floppy disk or via e-mail. Overall, using pop-up boxes enables students to read at considerable speed and differentiates by the extent to which they employ the original Web page or the copied Word document for their work.

Over time and with increasing confidence, students should rely less on the help provided by the Word document pop-up boxes. The potential danger here lies in the accessibility of the help – most students will be tempted to just access the translated word rather than deducting meaning from context. By asking them to keep a log of their progress, based on the number of boxes accessed for any particular text, they might feel more inclined to challenge themselves to improve on the number of boxes they had to use.

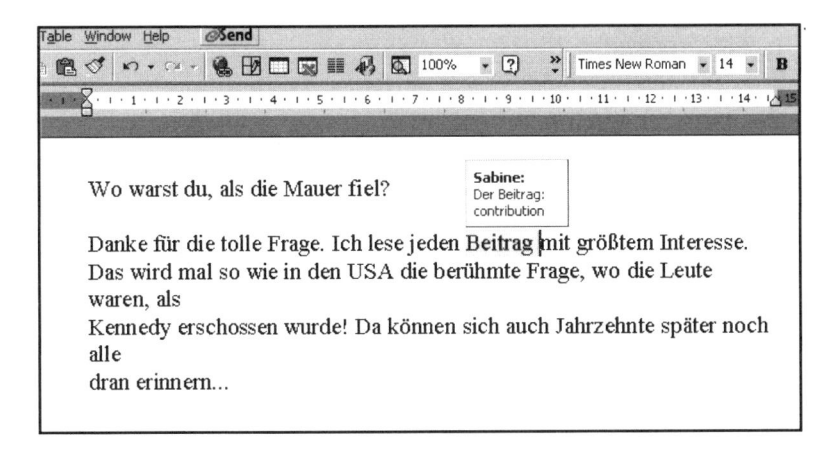

```
Wo warst du, als die Mauer fiel?        Sabine:
                                        Der Beitrag:
                                        contribution
Danke für die tolle Frage. Ich lese jeden Beitrag mit größtem Interesse.
Das wird mal so wie in den USA die berühmte Frage, wo die Leute
waren, als
Kennedy erschossen wurde! Da können sich auch Jahrzehnte später noch
alle
dran erinnern...
```

Once the vocabulary has been understood, it is highly likely that the students will read the text first and foremost with regards to its content, rather than any grammatical aspects it may cover – this is an important aspect of communicative language teaching and should be welcomed – after all, the text was written to impart knowledge, rather than to present grammar.

Introducing the grammar point

In general, it can be said that the more 'straightforward' the grammar is, the easier it will be to find a text which is suitable. At the German children's site of Geo (similar to the National Geographic), **www.geo.de/GEOlino,** every month a host of articles are presented on the Web in order to interest teenagers in history, anthropology, geography, politics, etc. Looking at recent articles, it is possible in a short space of time to find an article about two deaf teenagers which is largely (but not entirely) written in the third person plural in the present tense (see right). Introducing the text to the students, their first challenge is to 'spot the difference', i.e. identifying those structures which are written in the third person plural versus those that are not. Students may notice that, in German, the third person plural verb is identical to the infinitive, or they might need a bit of encouragement to do so. What might then follow is a comparison of other verb structures with the infinitive, leading to the knowledge that, once the infinitive has been learnt, first and third person plural take care of themselves. Example sentences regarding possible situations which require the third person plural – talking about parents, several siblings or friends, etc, follow. And while students contemplate the grammatical issues, they learn a lot about what it is like to be a teenager with a disability in Germany.

Once a grammar point has been introduced via a Web-based text, there is no reason why students should not use the same medium to practise it. Following on from the example above, students will be able to write a short paragraph about life as a teenager in Britain – easily adaptable according to the subject matter they wish to cover (such as a disability, the school system, a teenage model, etc) and combine the respective paragraphs on a web page (which, in turn, could be read by the year below). Furthermore, students may wish to take the content (as well as the grammar) further, by finding an online discussion group (**http://groups.yahoo.com** has details of examples), asking further questions about what it is like to be deaf and communicating with native speakers.

Taking it one step further

Once students have become used to using the Internet to explore grammar, they themselves (as well as the teacher) will become more and more aware of grammar as it is used on the Internet. As part of a long-term project, students could be asked to research a certain grammar point on the Internet individually and to present it to the rest of the class. To do this, it is once more possible to 'surf' until the opportunity presents itself. What is more likely, however, is the scenario that students are either given grammar points that are easy to find (a tense, imperatives, etc), or indeed, the website address of a suitable text, already

Advanced Pathfinder 5: *Getting to grips with grammar* – 49

found by the teacher. The first task here could be for the student to identify the grammar point in question, by going to the website and comparing structures and phrases with prior knowledge. The students are then asked to read up on 'their' grammar point, with the help of the coursebook, printed grammars, etc. Once they are more or less secure in their knowledge, they begin either to devise tasks for the other students, or to search the available grammatical material for whichever exercises they find best suited to teaching and learning grammar. Once all worksheets have been checked by the teacher to ensure they are correct, the students take over part of the lesson, giving a short lecture on the grammar point, speaking from first-hand experience about their own difficulties in getting to grips with it, and going through the devised worksheet with the group. It is likely that the group will find it refreshing to hear a frank account from a fellow student about finding a grammar point difficult, but 'tackling' and finally understanding it, rather than a teacher, who is perceived not to have any problems when it comes to the foreign language.

Finally, the work completed by the whole class can then be filed in the library of departmental materials, provided permission has been sought from copyright holders. Once the legal implications have been cleared, the tasks relating to the Internet-based texts may even be put on-line, creating a library of grammatical, content-related tasks accessible to the learners from home as well as from school. In this manner, students will be introduced to aspects of autonomous learning as well as peer-teaching, while retaining teacher support and guidance, helping to ensure that their final work is free from mistakes and increasing the students' confidence in their language use.

Conclusions to case study 3

Sabine's case study offers valuable suggestions on ways to choose and teach from Internet texts. Her suggestions for developing students' grammatical awareness, as in tasks such as 'spot the difference', relate to points made earlier about the importance of 'noticing' structures as a first step towards intake. But she also sets this activity in a wider context of growth and learning. Firstly, there is the motivation and increase in confidence of students for whom the Internet is a significant part of their lives. Secondly, there are the wider skills involved, going beyond language learning and affecting life-skills and future employment. Thirdly there are the possibilities for developing independence and autonomy in learning, a subject which will be explored further in Chapter 5.

key points

- Authentic texts present particular problems for the teacher who wishes to focus on a specific point of grammar.
- An initial stage in approaching the grammar of authentic texts must be tasks designed to promote recognition and awareness of grammar in context.
- The Internet is a valuable source of texts and material with immediate relevance.

5

Productive language, meaningful grammar practice, learner autonomy and peer teaching

Aims	This chapter aims to introduce discussion on: • grammar: process, practice and production; • types of grammar practice – from accuracy to fluency; • learner training and learner autonomy; • learning by teaching

We noted earlier (pp10–11) Schmidt's distinction between **input** (controlled by the teacher) and **intake,** which is 'that part of the input that the learner notices' (Schmidt 1990). We also referred (p11) to Johnson (1988) and his contention that it is often not knowledge which is at fault but lack of processing ability. An opportunity to process and practice may be the best way to give feedback, and not explanation.

This chapter will make suggestions for developing this phase of the teaching process but will also note the importance of student autonomy and peer teaching, and offer a case study on *Lernen durch Lehren* (learning by teaching). Students must take responsibility for their own learning. The teacher cannot do the learning for them.

Productive grammar

Chapter 4 developed ideas about receptive grammar and the importance of recognition preceding production. We now move to the practice or processing phase, where teachers with longer memories will remember, and wish to avoid, not just the solid grammatical exercises of the traditional approach but the mindless repetition of audio-lingual drills. By what sequence of more meaningful practice tasks can students internalise structures so that their correct use becomes near automatic? Ur (1988: 7–8) suggests that the phase of presentation (the recognition and awareness phase discussed in the previous chapter) should be followed by a phase where the grammatical item concerned is isolated from the context and explained. Then follows the practice phase 'whose aim is to cause the learners to absorb the structure thoroughly; or, to put it another way, to transfer what they know from short-term to long-term memory'. Ur (1996: 84) provides further detail for a sequence of grammar practice activities which moves from 'a very controlled and accuracy-oriented exercise at the beginning to a fluency activity giving opportunities for the free use of grammar in context at the end'.

Types of grammar practice: from accuracy to fluency   **Example**

▶ **Type 1: Awareness**

After the learners have been introduced to the structure, they are given opportunities to encounter it within some kind of discourse, and do a task that focuses their attention on its form and/or meaning.

Learners are given extracts from newspaper articles and asked to find and underline all the examples of the past tense that they can find.

▶ **Type 2: Controlled drills**

Learners produce examples of the structure: these examples are, however, predetermined by the teacher or textbook, and have to conform to very clear, closed-ended cues.

Write or say statements about John, modelled on the following example:
John drinks tea but he doesn't drink coffee.
a) like: ice cream/cake b) speak: English/Italian; c) enjoy: playing football/playing chess

▶ **Type 3: Meaningful drills**

Again, the responses are very controlled, but learners can make a limited choice of vocabulary.

Again in order to practise forms of the present simple tense:
Choose someone you know very well, and write down their name. Now compose true statements about them according to the following model:
He/She likes ice cream; OR He/She doesn't like ice cream.
a) enjoy: playing tennis b) drink: wine c) speak: Polish

▶ **Type 4: Guided, meaningful practice**

Learners form sentences of their own according to a set pattern, but exactly what vocabulary they use is up to them.

Practising conditional clauses, learners are given the cue 'If I had a million dollars', and suggest, in speech or writing, what they would do.

▶ **Type 5: (Structure-based) free sentence composition**

Learners are provided with a visual or situational cue and invited to compose their own responses; they are directed to use the structure.

A picture showing a number of people doing different things is shown to the class; they describe it using the appropriate tense.

▶ **Type 6: (Structure-based) discourse composition**

Learners hold a discussion or write a passage according to a given task; they are directed to use at least some examples of the structure within the discourse.

The class is given a dilemma situation ('You have seen a good friend cheating in an important test') and asked to recommend a solution. They are directed to include modals (might, should, must, can, could, etc) in their speech/writing.

▶ **Type 7: Free discourse**

As in Type 6, but the learners are given no specific direction to use the structure; however, the task situation is such that instances of it are likely to appear.

As in Type 6, but without the final direction.

Reproduced with permission from Penny Ur: *A course in language teaching* (p84)
© Cambridge University Press 1996

Each of these stages gives ample scope to the teacher of foreign languages to plan appropriate practice tasks. Ur's Type 1 (Awareness) was covered in the previous chapter when looking at ways to develop receptive grammar.

Following that, it should be noted that there must still be a place for formal and controlled exercises of a more 'traditional' kind. It may be that some of the current problems with students' lack of grammatical knowledge stem from pushing on too quickly from this stage. Such controlled tasks do not have to become pointless drilling. Repetitive practice tasks can still be made meaningful by relating to a real context or by introducing a gaming element. (See Martin Bowen Jones's case study, pp28 et seq). Following this controlled phase, the sequence introduces greater freedom at each stage. The controlled tasks first lay a foundation of knowledge and a start to facilitating **intake** which, as we have seen earlier (pp10–11), is the essential next step after initial input. Practice and processing then move towards tasks which are first guided then, increasingly, allow a freer response.

Ur's tabular sequence suggests oral as well as written activities, and grammatical accuracy is, of course, a feature of spoken as well as written communication. (See McLachlan, 2001.)

Language awareness and learner training

The idea of language awareness (LA) is widely known as a result of Eric Hawkins's work (Hawkins, 1984) although, sadly, the curriculum does not really allow for courses in LA as such. Raising consciousness about the workings of one's mother tongue might be seen as essential to an understanding of the way a foreign language works. Perhaps the otherwise laudable concentration on using the target language has led to a reduction in the chances to make explicit comparisons between first language and foreign language. Learner training is not so well known amongst teachers of foreign languages as language awareness, although the term is widely used in EFL. The idea of learner training is to help learners consider the factors that affect their learning and discover the learning strategies that suit them best. The emphasis is on **how** to learn rather than on **what** to learn. Learner training is based on the following two assumptions:

a) individuals learn in different ways and may use a variety of learning strategies at different times;

b) the more informed learners are about language and language learning, the more effective they will be at managing their own learning.

So learners need to be informed about the language (by language awareness activities), about language learning techniques (by experimentation and reflection) and about themselves as language learners (by self-assessment). Apart from their importance to individual language learners, this stress on self-awareness and learning how to learn echoes the themes of two of the Key Skills – Improving own language and performance, and Working with others.

Steps in learner training

Learner training should be seen as wider in scope than study skills, which involve the learner in specific tasks and activities, e.g. dictionary use and note taking. Ellis and Sinclair (1989) suggest skills training covering six skills, and within each skill, seven steps to develop learner autonomy:

Skills	Steps within each skill
(i) Extending vocabulary	(i) How do you feel about …?
(ii) Dealing with grammar	(ii) What do you know about …?
(iii) Listening	(iii) How well are you doing?
(iv) Speaking	(iv) What do you need to do next?
(v) Reading	(v) How do you prefer to learn/practise?
(vi) Writing	(vi) Do you need to build up your confidence?
	(vii) How do you organise …?

Such an approach stresses the autonomy of the learning process. Students take more responsibility for their own learning. The approach would also fit closely with the aims of the Key Skills mentioned above. Of course, one of the implications of such an approach is that teachers might have to face some undesirable opinions. Would one be resistant to students who said they learned best when always given the English alongside the target language? Or who preferred to write words down before being asked to retain them? We all tend to get stuck into our current thinking and to reject individual preferences which may be quite justified.

A number of contributions to the debate about teaching and learning grammar have pointed to the importance of learner-centred approaches. It is suggested that the learner's informal representation of linguistic knowledge may be more effective than traditional techniques based on linguists' description of language.

> *The basic source of information for an 'informal' pedagogical grammar is the learner himself; his own explanation of how he arrives at a given correct or incorrect linguistic form or structure. Needless to say, the teacher's informed explanation is crucial in cases where the learner fails to give a (plausible) explanation.*
> (Mohammed, 1995: 56)

We have made the point, in discussing learner training, that autonomy means that learners accept responsibility for their own learning – a difficult challenge and one which may well be resisted. But in acquiring awareness of grammar and applying the rules, rates of intake are so different among members of a group of students, that some aspects of an individual learning programme are essential. Little (1994: 83) has made out a convincing case for learner autonomy in foreign language study.

> *[...] there is a crucial sense in which all learning is internal to the learner. However much we consult with our learners about learning targets and how best to achieve them [...] we cannot control what goes on inside each learner's head. What is more, learners require time and psychological space in which to learn; and if we are too insistently interventionist in our pedagogical practice we can all too easily deprive them of that time and space.*

Rendall (1998: 67) also makes a powerful argument for responding to individual needs. Although she is concerned with students pre-GCSE, her points are just as relevant to more advanced learners:

> *If [our pupils] can't do something, it could be because:*
> - *we are asking them to do it too soon;*
> - *we have not given them enough time to absorb the new work;*
> - *we have not helped them find an effective way of learning;*
> - *we haven't taken into account their own hypotheses on language and language learning or uncovered any possible misconceptions;*
> - *we haven't asked them where the problem lies.*

One way of encouraging a chance for individuals to explore a problem for themselves, rather than endlessly going over adjectival endings or the formation of a past tense, is for teachers to prepare grammar worksheets which set out the key features of the point in question in user-friendly English and give the student a programmed sequence of activities. The teacher need only intervene when the student runs up against a problem.

Learning by teaching

An interesting, and rather different, angle on learner-centred methods is provided by the approach known as *Lernen durch Lehren* (learning by teaching) (LDL). In 1996, Konrad Huber, now a Headteacher in Munich, completed a research project on this approach as part of work leading to a Master's degree. The following case study gives some details of the approach with more specific reference to the teaching of grammar. The study concerns German pupils learning English.

Although younger than students preparing for A level, and the grammar points dealt with are at a more elementary level, the principles outlined here are of particular interest for the developing autonomy of the more mature students in Years 12 and 13.

case study 4	**Learning by teaching – the way towards more student participation in foreign languages?** by Konrad Huber

The concept *Lernen durch Lehren* (LDL) was first developed and tested in the eighties by Jean-Pol Martin, a senior lecturer for the teaching of French at the University of Eichstätt in Germany and responsible for various research projects connected with LDL (Martin 1985 and 1994). The idea of this concept is to move away from traditional class teaching where almost every step in a lesson is focused and concentrated on the teacher. Martin called for a radical change and devised a concept whereby students are enabled to organise more and more of the teaching and learning process themselves.

Basic principles

One basic principle of the concept is that, after a period of introduction, the teacher enables the students to take over traditional tasks of the teacher, such as directing a reading exercise, correcting and checking homework, introducing new vocabulary or introducing new grammatical items. The teacher makes sure that all students are involved in the teaching, helps with the preparations and corrects the material the students devise for their own teaching. During the lessons the teacher only intervenes if there are questions that cannot be answered by the respective **peer teacher** (the student, who is involved in the teaching process). In most LDL lessons one student functions as the presenter. He or she speaks some sentences between the different steps in a lesson and calls the peer teachers when it is their turn. A plan showing the structure of the lesson helps him or her not to forget parts of the lesson. Martin, who has been using the concept with a French group at a German *Gymnasium* for many years, compares the LDL concept with traditional teaching and claims that it gives the students much wider opportunities than any other way of teaching to use and practise the new language.

Social and psychological aspects

Apart from these linguistic and didactic advantages of the concept, social and psychological aspects play an important role when students function as teachers. Legutke, an important protagonist of Martin's way of teaching and learning, supports this view and claims that the expansion of the learner's role into that of a teacher has not only a positive impact on the motivation of the individual, but also on the whole group, which tends to function more as a community of learners (Legutke 1993). While presenting new structures and vocabulary in front of the class, the students find themselves again and again in new situations. Martin and other LDL teachers claim that after a period of introduction the students act confidently and without any problems in front of the class. Very soon there is an atmosphere of solidarity between the students which on the whole enhances and supports the learning process. Experiments show that students learn much more effectively if they reflect about their own learning process.

While planning their own presentations of new material, the students have to explore a section of lesson content themselves and consider carefully how they want to explain the new structures so that the other students understand what they are teaching. They also have to check whether the information is understood and devise appropriate exercises to do this.

Structure of research project

The main aim of my small research project, which was carried out in two schools in Germany, was to find out:

- how the principles of LDL can be put into practice;
- whether Martin's concept is feasible and effective;
- how the pupils react to the implementation of this new way of teaching.

The classroom language throughout the project was the target language (English). The research project was mainly concentrated on three areas:

- the introduction of new vocabulary by students;
- the introduction of new grammatical structures by students;
- learning at individual workplaces.

The project was carried out at two *Realschulen* which are separate schools on a level between the *Hauptschule* (secondary modern school) and the *Gymnasium* (traditional grammar school). The test groups consisted of 22 boys aged 13 and 14 who had been taught English as a foreign language for two years. The LDL concept was used throughout the six weeks of the project, for which 14 English lessons of 45 minutes were allocated. The content of the unit was divided into small parts so that all pupils were actively involved in the peer teaching.

Introduction of new grammatical structures

We wanted to test whether pupils in their third year of English are able to explain new grammatical structures in the target language. As it was the first time that the pupils had to introduce the grammar themselves a relatively easy aspect of grammar was chosen – the regular and irregular plural of nouns. After correcting homework, which at this stage was completely organised by the students, one peer teacher started with the repetition of the regular plural of nouns. He put a transparency on the overhead projector and covered it up. Then he pointed at one student and said: 'This is one student, but how many students are in class?' He asked several students and they replied: 'There are 22 students in class'. Then the peer teacher showed this sentence on the transparency and asked the rest of the class for the rule. As soon as the first student said: 'When there is more than one student you have to add an -s', the peer teacher uncovered the rule and said 'Well done!'.

Then the next peer teacher came to the front of the class. He had to explain the irregular plural of nouns ending with an -f. He, therefore, had brought a leaf with him and followed the same principle. He used the same method for 'knife–knives' and the rest of the class had to find the rule. The students did not seem to have any problems with the explanation of the new grammatical structure and answered: 'When a word ends with an -f it becomes -ves in the plural'. After this he continued in the same way with the example 'potato–potatoes' and let the rest of the class find the corresponding rule. He illustrated this example with two small potatoes which he had in a bag. The next peer teacher explained the irregular plural of 'box–boxes' and 'teddy–teddies'. All three students who had to introduce and explain the new structures in the target language had no problems in doing so. They all had two days for preparing their part and were allowed to ask the teacher for advice. Apart from this assistance the students were given no other instructions. It was interesting to see that all the peer teachers used the target language all the way through without referring to the mother tongue. There was an exciting atmosphere and the class applauded after each performance. The ideas to bring along potatoes, boxes, leaves and even a teddy reflected the creative talents of the students which are often not engaged in ordinary lessons.

The rest of the lesson was used to practise the different ways of building the plural. The students had prepared a grammar game for which the class was divided into two groups. One student, who was the referee, showed sentences on a transparency in which the correct plural was missing. One student from each group had to run to the blackboard and write the correct word on the board as quickly as possible. The group with the first correct solution scored a point. This exercise had two purposes. On the one hand the students practised the spelling of the different plurals – which usually creates problems for most of the students – and on the other hand they had the opportunity to repeat some of the vocabulary of the unit.

Conclusions to case study 4

Konrad's use of LDL as a teaching technique clearly increases students' involvement in their own learning. Motivation is enhanced, both for the individual and the group, and the students' own creativity is brought into play.

key points
- Following on from recognition as a prerequisite to grammar learning, the processing phase of grammar teaching aims to transfer awareness into productive knowledge.
- There is a spectrum of grammar practice tasks stretching from consciousness-raising through controlled practice to arrive at free discourse.
- Learner training, learner autonomy and peer teaching should be key features of a course involving grammar learning in the A level course.

6

Grammar in the AS and A2 examinations – preparing, performing and assessing

Aims	This chapter aims to introduce discussion on: • the place of grammar in AS/A2 specifications; • the range of exam tasks involving grammatical knowledge; • preparation of students for examination tasks; • types of assessment of grammatical performance.

The new AS/A2 specifications were introduced for courses starting in 2000 and AS was first examined in 2001. The specifications were constructed within strict criteria and guidelines laid down by the Qualifications and Assessment Authority (QCA). (For details, see Neather 2001). At the outset, it may be helpful to state once more the four Assessment Objectives (AO) of the specifications so as to explain later references in this chapter.

Candidates should be able to:

A01 understand and respond, in speech and writing, to spoken language;
A02 understand and respond, in speech and writing, to written language;
A03 show knowledge of and apply accurately the grammar and syntax prescribed in the specification;
A04 demonstrate knowledge and understanding of aspects of the chosen society.

There are two elements in the new specifications which focus on grammatical accuracy and appear to give a new emphasis to grammar following a period when grammar had appeared to be in retreat. Firstly, there are lists of prescribed structures laid down by QCA, an innovation in foreign language syllabuses at A level. The lists are presented in the Edexcel specification, for example, with the following preamble:

> *AS and Advanced GCE students will be expected to have studied closely the grammatical system and structures of the [...] language during their course. In the examination they will be required to use actively and accurately grammar and structures appropriate to the tasks set, drawn from the following list. The grammar listed here is prescribed by the QCA subject criteria for Modern Foreign Languages.*

Secondly, the third assessment objective – AO3 – for the new examination is specific in giving a 25% weighting to grammatical features, at each level.

However, we need to be clear about the significance of both these claims to rigorous assessment of grammar and accuracy.

Lists of grammatical structures

Question: What should be the point of including a list of grammatical structures in an examination specification?

Answer: An A level syllabus should be specific about testing certain key structures, receptively or productively, rather than leaving them to chance use in an essay or other short piece of writing.

Question: Do the structure lists in the current specifications meet the requirements of that answer?

Answer: No, because they play a minimal part in the setting of papers and no structure is considered so essential that it must be tested.

One can assume that the usual range of examination tasks will cover the general areas of agreements, conjugations, word order, etc. But it might reasonably be considered that an A level syllabus should be specific about testing certain key structures, receptively or productively, rather than leaving them to chance use in an essay or other short piece of writing. For example, receptively, the ability to recognise the force of a conditional sentence could be targeted by questions testing this awareness. Productively, the ability to use certain tenses might be **required.** If this train of thought were pursued, it would have a significant effect on test techniques by requiring tasks where structures could be specified. A decision would then have to be taken as to the coverage of such key structures in a single examination, or how often such structures should be sampled over a period of time. The key to such questions is whether there is any agreement about what an A level candidate **must** be able to do in the foreign language. The conclusion is that a chance was missed by the language lists in the current specifications. They cause teachers a deal of worry, especially because of the extent of the AS lists. But there is no need for undue concern because, apart from avoiding the very few items in the A2 lists when setting AS papers, examiners need pay no attention to the lists. They are simply a list of things that might crop up, as they might in any text, and which a candidate can probably avoid using productively.

Assessment of AO3

The assessment objective AO3 is ambiguously phrased. The apparent distinction between grammar and syntax is unclear. One's usual understanding is that constituent parts of the umbrella term grammar are word grammar (morphology) and sentence grammar (syntax). Accepting it at face value, however the AO seems to say 'get your endings and your word order right!'. But a glance at the assessment grids of the various Examination Boards shows that a much wider interpretation has been placed on the phrasing of the AO. The words are interpreted to mean not just accuracy but the whole range of criteria which can be grouped under the general heading 'Quality of language'. Here are some examples.

Edexcel AS Unit 1 Listening & Writing

Out of 50 marks for this paper, 4 are given for AO3, defined as 'Quality of language', and applied globally to performance on two personal responses (30–40 words each), to a recorded stimulus. The highest mark (4) is given for the performance described as follows:

> *Excellent communication. Language almost always fluent, varied and appropriate. Very high level of accuracy.*

For 3 marks, the candidate's performance should have the following characteristics:

> *Good communication. Shows a good variety of lexis and structures. Errors usually minor.*

As is often the case with descriptive criteria, the phrasing is imprecise until examiners are shown examples and have sample scripts to mark. Then, terms like 'high level' and 'minor' become clear. More to the point of the argument presented here is the broad interpretation of the phrasing of AO3. What seemed to be an emphasis on grammatical knowledge and accuracy has, in practice, come to include communication, fluency, lexis.

AQA AS Unit 1 Listening, Reading & Writing

The example from AQA shows more direct reference to the phrasing of AO3.

In Part C, 10 marks are awarded globally to a set of answers to seven questions. Although the mark grid is introduced by a reference to 'Quality of language' (AO3), a warning note is then included: 'Where there is nothing of relevance in the answer to the question set no marks will be awarded for 'Knowledge of grammar.' This clearly means that in the AQA interpretation 'Quality of language' and 'Knowledge of grammar' are seen to be synonymous. In this scheme, the highest marks, 9–10, are given for the following performance:

> *The manipulation of most structures is good and examples of complex language are frequently used. There are still a few inaccuracies, but these tend to occur in more complex structures.*

Clearly, some clarification ('frequently [...] few') would be needed at the standardisation meeting for examiners, but this criterion does contain some key words in the assessment of grammar: manipulation of structures; complex language; inaccuracies.

OCR AS Unit 3 Reading & Writing

Here is one final example of a mark grid from OCR aimed at the same sort of performance.

Candidates must write 100–150 words in response to a text of around 300 words. They are awarded marks for Comprehension (10), Response (10) and Quality of language (10). The highest level of achievement for the last of these (9–10) is described as follows:

> *High and consistent level of accuracy. Mainly minor errors. The overall impression is one of competence. Confident and correct use of a varied range of structures.*

So the criteria selected by OCR are: accuracy; variety and range; and also competence – a not very precise term which the Principal Examiner would no doubt explain at a standardisation meeting.

These examples are representative of the mark schemes included throughout the specifications of the various Boards. At the very least, they demonstrate a lack of agreement as to what AO3 actually means in practice. In addition, the grids represent a style of marking which has become standard since the GCSE was introduced in 1988 and where the emphasis is on a positive response to the general quality of performance rather than on a negative concern with error.

There are examples in the AS and A2 papers of tests which target grammar in a more specific way, and these will be considered in the following section.

Preparing students for exam tasks

As an approach to the preparation for exam tasks, we shall first refer back to the discussion on receptive and productive grammar in Chapters 4 and 5, and in particular to the summary on p53. The range of tasks in Listening and Reading papers may be classified within that same framework and are divided here into three main categories:

1 Tasks requiring recognition of structures but no production
2 Tasks requiring more precise recognition of structures and/or some production
3 Tasks requiring controlled or free production

1 Tasks requiring recognition of structures but no production

There is a range of non-verbal tasks which are not assessed for AO3 and where grammatical knowledge does not have to be indicated by productive use of the language. Nevertheless, recognition of grammatical features is required. These tasks include variations on the True/False test format and other kinds of multiple choice tests.

> **Example 1 (extract): True/False with correction where required**
> (From WJEC French AS, Unit 3, June 2001)

The text is presented in poster style, so the following is a single extract to illustrate the choice to be made by the student:

> **Les résidences universitaires**
>
> C'est le moyen le moins cher pour se loger. Pour 710 F par mois, vous disposez d'une chambre équipée d'un bureau. La cuisine, les douches et la télé sont communes ...
>
> Indiquez si les phrases suivantes sont vraies (V) ou fausses (F). Corrigez les phrases qui sont fausses.
>
> (i) Les résidences universitaires sont très chères. | V | F |
>
> *Correction si nécessaire*
>
> ....
>
> (ii) Chaque chambre universitaire est équipée d'une cuisine et d'une douche. | V | F |
>
> *Correction si nécessaire*
>
> ....

© WJEC

Both these items are false. The mark scheme indicates two marks for each, whereas answers which are True receive one mark. One can assume, therefore that there is a mark for indicating False and a mark for an answer communicating the correct information, with no penalty for grammatical error in the answer. To answer the questions requires not just understanding of the lexis but also recognition of the superlative *le moins cher* in (i) and recognition of the feminine plural of the adjective *communes* in (ii).

Example 2: Find exact equivalent in text
(From OCR French AS sample papers, Unit 3, 2000)

This style of text is sometimes concerned only with lexical items. The following example also requires some grammatical insight.

> Il est minuit ... Rungis s'éveille. 00heures les premiers camions déchargent. 2h du matin: la marée monte. Le marché aux poissons est le plus matinal. Les pavillons des produits carnés, eux, accueillent les acheteurs dès 4h. Suivent les produits laitiers à 5h, les fruits, légumes et fleurs à 6h.
>
> Trouvez dans le texte l'équivalent EXACT des expressions ci-dessous. Les expressions se trouvent dans le bon ordre.
>
> (a) (le marché) devient plus animé
> (b) celui qui ouvre le premier
> (c) le beurre, le fromage etc.

© OCR

Advanced Pathfinder 5: *Getting to grips with grammar* – 67

Of course, some answers are largely lexical, e.g. the recognition of *laitiers*. But *ouvre le premier* requires recognition of the superlative in *le plus matinal*.

Preparation for tests of this type requires grammar recognition exercises as described on pp42–43.

2 Tasks requiring more precise recognition of structures and/or some production

A further range of task-types require skills of recognition and awareness of specific structures in context, and may also demand some limited production of items, as in the following examples.

■ **Example 3: Gap-filling and sentence-completion**
(From CCEA French AS, Unit 2, June 2001)

This task is the first of three test items following a text entitled *Un chauffeur de camion, arrêté par la police, raconte son aventure.*

Complétez les phrases suivantes en employant le mot ou la phrase qui convient:

irrégulier	tout de suite	rendu
renversé	important	tout à coup
s'ennuyaient	son patron	le client
son copain	le chauffeur	couraient

(i)   Avant de partir, François consulte toujours …
(ii) Il a remarqué quelque chose d' … en regardant son camion sur l'autoroute.
(iii) Il a vu des gens qui …
(iv) François décide de contacter les autorités …
(v)   Les autorités ont … les produits confisqués quelques jours plus tard.
(vi) C'est … qui s'est mis en colère parce qu'il a dû attendre sa marchandise pendant deux semaines.

The six marks awarded for this task are for AO2, that is 'understand and respond, in speech and writing, to written language'. But the fact that there is no mark for AO3 should not disguise the fact that this is also a task of providing specific items of grammar. There are four possibilities for sentence (i), for which the answer must be a noun preceded by a determiner. The answer might most reasonably be *le client* or *son patron*, and a check back to the text is needed to confirm. The text says: *Avant de partir, il a suivi les instructions habituelles de son employeur*. So the key knowledge required by the student in preparing for such a task is, firstly, to isolate the only grammatical forms which can possibly fill the gap; secondly, to scan the text for a sentence confirming the information.

Example 4: Match halves of sentences
(From UCLES legacy French A level, November 2000)

This task-type has been used in both AS and A2. This task refers back to a text on contemporary attitudes to marriage.

Trouvez dans la liste de fins de phrase en bas celle qui termine correctement chaque début de phrase selon le sens du texte. Attention! Il y a plus de fins de phrase que de débuts. Vous ne pouvez utiliser une fin de phrase qu'une seule fois. La première case a déjà été remplie à titre d'exemple.

(i)	(ii)	(iii)	(iv)	(v)	(vi)
B					

Débuts de phrase

(i) Le mariage est devenu moins fréquent pendant les années 70
(ii) Les habitants des campagnes ne sont pas portés vers l'union libre
(iii) Beaucoup de femmes craignent le mariage
(iv) Dans le passé les couples vivaient ensemble un certain temps
(v) Aujourd'hui les jeunes préfèrent l'union libre au mariage
(vi) On remarque que le nombre de couples vivant en union libre est plus élevé

Fins de phrase

A … parce que c'est un mode de vie plus adapté au travail et aux aspirations actuelles.
B … parce que les jeunes ont commencé a vivre ensemble.
C … principalement dans la capitale et les grandes villes.
D … parce qu'il est synonyme d'absence de liberté.
E … pour être sûrs qu'ils s'entendraient bien une fois mariés.
F … parce que ce mode de vie compliquerait la question d'héritage.
G … parce que l'importance des diplômes est capitale.
H … parce que l'arrivée d'un enfant complique la chose.

© OCR

There are two stages involved in this task. Firstly, students can exclude any sentence in the right-hand column which does not connect grammatically with the opening provided. Then, the correct half of a sentence must be chosen to fit in with the sense of the preceding text. So in this example, grammatical connections alone are not enough. Sentence (i) could be followed grammatically by any of the sequence except E.

Example 5: Grammatical cloze test
(OCR French AS, Unit 3, June 2001)

OCR AS Unit 3 allocates 15 AO3 marks to a very specific task focusing on key grammatical items. Candidates have a text of 150 words, to which they respond in writing. They are then faced with a series of sentences requiring a gap to be filled by a correct grammatical item chosen from three possibilities. As with other examples given here, understanding of the text is not a vital element in this task, as is clear from the following example.

Complétez les phrases ci-dessous en cochant (✔) la case appropriée.

Exemple:
La question est de savoir s'il est nécessaire   A à
                                                 B de ✔
                                                 C pour   réguler l'internet.

(a) On se demande   A qu'est-ce qui
                         B ce qui
                         C ce qu'   il faut faire pour maîtriser l'Internet.

(b) Les autorités s'en occupent à partir du moment   A où
                                                     B quand
                                                     C auquel   la vie privée est
                                                                  menacée.

(c) Estelle Halliday a déposé une plainte   A parce que
                                             B pour
                                             C à cause de   certaines images.

© OCR

In such a test there is no escaping the need to be precise about a specific structure. But of course it is still the case that this is grammar as **recognition.** The students are not required to **produce** structures of their own choosing in such a task. Although this style of task is common in TEFL tests, there are teachers who dislike it because it actually brings the student face to face with errors.

3 Tasks requiring controlled or free production

The third type of test-type is where production of structures is required, either in a relatively controlled way or by more extended writing.

Example 6: Completing sentences
(Edexcel German AS, Unit 1, June 2001)

The example here is taken from an Edexcel listening paper. The candidates listen to a spoken text using the Walkman mode, i.e. they can replay as often as they like. A section of the transcript of the listening text is first given, then the first three examples of the task. The suggested answers from the mark-scheme are given in brackets for each sentence.

Sie hören jetzt ein Gespräch mit einer 75-Jährigen. Ergänzen Sie dann die folgenden Sätze auf Deutsch, so dass sie dem Hörtext entsprechen.

A   Frau Kobis, Sie wohnen mit der Familie Ihres Sohnes unter einem Dach und haben Ihre Enkel mit aufwachsen gesehen. Wenn Sie mal Ihre Generation mit der Ihrer Enkel vergleichen, können Sie da irgendwelche Unterschiede sehen?

B   Tja, also wenn ich so an meine Jugend zurückdenke – unsere Erziehung war nicht so frei, das muss ich schon sagen. Wir konnten nicht alles haben, was wir wollten. Die Situation war wirtschaftlich nicht so gut wie jetzt.

(a)   Frau Kobis wohnt _____ (bei ihrem Sohn/mit (bei) der Familie ihres Sohnes)

(b)   Frau Kobis meint, dass Kinder heute _____ (freier sind/es besser/mehr haben)

(c)   Sie hatte in ihrer Jugend weniger _____ (Geld/Chancen/Sachen)

© Edexcel

It is obvious that the mark-scheme expects short answers, which is not surprising, considering that each sentence is allocated just one mark. It should also be borne in mind that this is a listening text and, if candidates can retain chunks of the original, it would, no doubt, be acceptable. So, a candidate who completes the first sentence: *mit der Familie Ihres Sohnes unter einem Dach* would no doubt get the mark.

Example 7: Rewriting sentences in your own words
(CCEA French AS, Unit 2, June 2001)

The following task is clearly a further step up the production ladder. Although the student has a prompt, the actual sentence written is in his/her own words.

The task follows on from the same text quoted in Example 3 (p68).

Exprimez autrement les expressions soulignées dans les phrases suivantes. Écrivez des phrases complètes.

Modèle: François <u>est chauffeur de camion</u> depuis 27 ans.
   François conduit un camion depuis 27 ans.

(i)   J'ai dû réparer un pneu.

   ....

(ii) Il n'y avait personne à l'intérieur du camion.

   ....

(iii) Je n'ai rien contre les clandestins.

   ....

© CCEA

The task is marked out of 5, all for AO3. In contrast to the itemised mark-schemes seen in the above examples, this task is marked **globally** with a language mark allocated to the whole performance. It is worth quoting the CCEA mark scheme for this task (see below).

Assistant examiners should review responses to the three tasks and allocate an overall mark based on the grid below.

Band	Description of performance	Marks
3	French manipulated accurately. Good sensitivity to idiom; syntactic awareness. Competent command of relevant vocabulary.	4–5
2	Adequate evidence of ability to use vocabulary and structures correctly. Some idiomatic awareness.	2–3
1	Vocabulary and structures limited. Little idiomatic awareness.	0–1

Possible candidate responses:

(i) J'ai été obligé de réparer un pneu.

(ii) Personne n'était dans le camion/à l'intérieur du camion.

(iii) Je ne déteste pas les clandestins.

As was mentioned earlier, grids do seem to overflow beyond the bounds of the simple descriptive statement of AO3. Vocabulary and idiom are drawn into the assessment of this task, which basically just demands that the student find alternative structures to those given.

Questions on a text are the obvious and most common text-type requiring understanding of the grammar of the text and some ability to manipulate the language. There is no need to give examples of this common test-type, but it is worth noting that there is some debate as to how much lifting from the stimulus text may be permitted and to what extent the answer should show a capacity to manipulate the language.

Example 8: Transfer from English into the foreign language
(OCR Spanish AS, Unit 1 sample papers, 2000)

The QCA criteria require transfer between English and the foreign language and vice versa. Transfer may be a small piece of actual translation or a piece to be rendered in the student's own words, as in the following example.

OCR devote part of AS Unit 1 to a sequence of business activities, requiring translation of a letter from a foreign contact and then a return note on the lines of the following example:

> *Poco después, la señora Mary Nightingale, Directora del Esplanade Hotel, te pasa este memorándum. Escribe la carta que le pide: puede utilizar frases y vocabulario de la carta de la Sra Suárez que acaba de traducir. Escribe tu carta en la página siguiente.*
>
> > Please write to Ms Suárez: thank her for her letter of 23 June. Say that our hotel has several rooms of the size she needs, and we will have space for her group in the last two weeks of August 2001. Tell her we enclose the information she requested. Say if she has not already made a final decision on the dates for the visit, we recommend she makes a provisional reservation as soon as possible.

© OCR

Candidates are given the following page as a start to their letter:

> Esplanade Hotel,
> Grand Parade,
> Southsea,
> Portsmouth.
>
> 27 de junio d 2000
>
> Sra. Alicia Suárez,
> Asociación de Cámaras de Comercio del País Vasco,
> Paseo de Cantabria,
> Bilbao,
> Spain
>
> Estimada Sra. Suárez:
> Le damos las gracias por su carta del 23 junio. Tenemos el placer de informarle que ...

Candidates are encouraged to use their own structures, rather than translate, and they may also draw from the preceding letter received from the Spanish correspondent. This is therefore a carefully guided writing task with structures that have been, to some extent, preselected. This piece of work is marked out of 10, according to descriptive criteria. So the top band scores 9–10 for:

> *High and consistent level of accuracy. Mainly minor errors. The overall impression is one of competence. Confident and correct use of a varied range of structures.*

From this first step in guided writing, productive tasks cover a spectrum starting with a limited stimulus and guidelines, as in Example 9 below.

Example 9: Directed writing task
(Edexcel French AS, Unit 2, June 2001)

> **Portefeuille trouvé**
>
> > Hier après-midi, un retraité qui habite notre commune depuis 3 ans a trouvé, en promenant son chien, un portefeuille. En citoyen bien honnête, il a immédiatement apporté l'objet trouvé au commissariat. Le portefeuille en question contient de nombreuses choses qui doivent bien manquer à son propriétaire.
> >
> > Si vous pensez que ce portefeuille est le vôtre, présentez-vous au commissariat ou écrivez-nous en nous apportant des preuves qu'il est bien à vous.
>
> Vous avez lu cette annonce dans le journal de la région où vous passez vos vacances. Comme vous avez perdu votre portefeuille, vous décidez d'écrire au commissariat. **En 140 à 160 mots, écrivez en français une lettre dont le contenu est bien clairement situé dans le contexte d'un pays francophone.** Vous devez:
> - Dire quand vous avez perdu votre portefeuille
> - Raconter de qui s'est passé pour expliquer cette perte
> - Décrire en détail le contenu du portefeuille en donnant des précisions
> - Expliquer comment et où le commissariat peut vous contacter si le portefeuille est bien le vôtre

© Edexcel

It is clear that the text is of limited value to the candidate in constructing the answer, but the accompanying directions are essential. Not only do they give precision to the content of the candidate's piece, but they insist on certain grammatical features, notably, the fact that the piece must be in the past tense.

Following on from this guided composition, the final stage is free composition, right up to the essays to be written in the Texts and Topics paper of A2.

key points

- Exam tasks can be seen as following the teaching sequence described earlier, where grammar is encountered firstly as recognition and awareness and subsequently as production and usage.
- Non-verbal tasks may frequently require a recognition of grammar in context.
- A range of specific, itemised tasks do require precise knowledge of endings and inflections, even if the student does not need to show that knowledge productively.
- More extended productive writing tasks are marked according to global descriptive criteria which offer positive statements, taking the whole performance into account and accepting a certain amount of error.
- The interpretation of the assessment of grammatical knowledge (according to Assessment Objective 3) varies between the Boards and includes a number of indicators besides accuracy.

Conclusions

We must get away from any idea that teaching grammar is something that requires an apology. If we understand grammar as patterns underlying all language, then teaching an insight into those patterns and the rules that govern them is always important. For students preparing for A level examinations, such an insight is essential.

But the traditional view of grammar teaching in the A level course has been transformed by a number of significant changes.

Changing views of language

Firstly there are changes in the way language is viewed. Language teaching at A level is centred around topics and authentic texts, and has communicative competence as its primary aim. That aim must necessarily also include grammatical competence, but the formal, rule-based element in language teaching is set within a new context. The range of skills to be achieved by the A level student goes far beyond formal correctness in written production.

Grammar should now be seen as, firstly, recognition and noticing of grammatical features. This awareness is a first and necessary step before moving on to forms of grammatical production.

Changes in the composition of the sixth form

Secondly there are changes in the composition of the sixth form. The evidence of Chapters 2 and 3 of this book shows how the range of ability of students entering the sixth form has changed. The traditional A level course fitted into a unified scheme which progressed from O level to A level to a university language course. Students post-GCSE have a different knowledge base and may well decide not to continue with the language beyond AS level. So the teacher's initial approach has to take account of the mixed ability nature of the sixth form, the need for differentiation and the varying aims for future language study.

It is also the case that students are now used to more personal choice and autonomy in their studies. Developments such as key skills and coursework involving personal research and the whole ethos of the times lead to the conclusion that students must be given the chance to investigate their own learning strategies. This may be truer for grammar learning than for any other part of their studies, since the need to internalise a system of rules takes time and is a variable process for each individual. It is no accident that all contributors to this book, without any collaboration on this point, stressed the need for learner autonomy.

Changes in examinations

The new pattern of AS and A2 exams has significantly affected foreign language teaching in a number of ways. When considering the testing of grammar in the exams, it is important to note that grammatical knowledge and understanding are not only tested by Assessment Objective 3. The examples given in Chapter 6 show that recognition of grammar and structure is an important part of other assessment objectives. In fact, the range of tasks presented in the exam mirrors the sequence of teaching suggested in this book: a progression from recognition and awareness, through controlled production of specific items to arrive at free expression assessed positively by global performance descriptors.

Chapter 1 of this book started by quoting sages such as Comenius and Erasmus and making the statement, ' In discussions about the teaching of grammar, there is nothing new under the sun'. It is hardly likely, therefore, that the present author could claim to have reached definitive conclusions. He can only claim that important issues have been aired, significant factors explored and a number of illuminating case studies have given food for thought. Maybe, with a book on grammar teaching, the only conclusion is to quote Eliot:

> *We shall not cease from exploration*
> *And the end of all our exploring*
> *Will be to arrive where we started*
> *And know the place for the first time.*
>
> *Four quartets:* 'Little Gidding'

Appendix 1: postgraduate student difficulties in learning grammar

PGCE students of MFL are a very varied bunch – varied in age, language experience and, of course, in grammatical knowledge. The changing priorities in schools with regard to the place of grammar teaching were described in Chapter 1. Teacher trainees who have lived through those changes are likely to have encountered little formal grammar in their English classes or GCSE courses in MFL. Despite 'remedial' and 'refresher' courses on entering the sixth form and starting their university course, postgraduate students often start their teacher-training course with gaps and uncertainties in their grammatical knowledge. Even though they may be fluent speakers and competent writers, they will still find themselves put on the spot when they have to give an immediate response to questions from pupils. As new entrants to the teaching profession they may be faced with particular problems when asked to teach grammar to A level students. It is important, therefore, that we take into account grammatical knowledge among teacher trainees.

The following short piece by Debra Myhill reports on her research with English PGCE students. She makes some distinctions between the attitudes to grammar of MFL and English students, but many of her significant points about grammatical knowledge and understanding are relevant to foreign linguists as well as those intending to be teachers of English. This is partly because foreign linguists do need to understand the grammar of their mother tongue if they are to help pupils make comparisons and raise awareness. Also, the field of grammar is so all embracing that, as Debra puts it, 'so much grammatical understanding relies on other grammatical understandings'.

***

Changes in the National Curriculum for English (2000), reinforced in the Framework for English at Key Stage 3, have significantly raised the profile of grammar and metalanguage in the context of first language (L1) English lessons in the UK. In particular, the designation of precise learning objectives for pupils at word, sentence and text level – many of which specify metalinguistic understanding – means that it is no longer possible to teach English and avoid teaching grammar. These curriculum changes have created a new national imperative for teachers of English to understand grammar sufficiently to be able to teach it with confidence. For students training to be L1 English teachers, the national standards which have to be met in order to achieve Qualified Teacher Status (DfES 2002) now require that students *'have secure knowledge and understanding'* of the subject they intend to teach, including the knowledge specified by the National Curriculum.

For these postgraduate L1 English students, learning grammar in an already intensive one-year professional training course is a considerable challenge. Psychologically, they frequently approach the endeavour with conflicting values and motivations. On the one hand, they have been academically successful in English without any obvious need for metalinguistic knowledge, and thus they begin the course with a somewhat sceptical attitude about the value of learning and teaching grammar. On the other hand, they are acutely aware of their need to acquire the relevant understanding in order to meet the national standards and pass the course. This awareness is often coupled with a sense of failure at not knowing about the grammar of their own language already and an indignant condemnation of their own school curriculum for not introducing it.

However, setting aside the psychological 'baggage' which shapes students' attitude to learning about grammar, students' early encounters with grammar are often made difficult because of their weak conceptualisation of what grammar is. Their schemata for grammar are often rather weak and hazy, dominated by notions of correctness. Many students conceptualise grammar as a monolithic structure, and are unaware that there are multiple grammars: indeed, there is a fusing of the concept of grammar as something which describes how language works with the metalanguage which is used to describe it. For MFL or EFL students, contrastive linguistics may draw attention to the different grammar systems of different languages; but for L1 students it is the different grammars of written and spoken English which are more significant. Superimposed over this is a view, acquired from public debates about grammar, that grammar is about error and correction, the moral corrective to the sins of the word. Keith sums this up well when he notes the tendency *'to make the study of grammar ... a prescribed antibiotic!'* (Keith 1994). From this standpoint, students' own learning about grammar is coloured by a conceptualisation of right and wrong, a notion which creates an inordinate fear of being wrong and a crippling desire for rules. They find it difficult to reconcile the apparent mathematical precision of grammatical terminology with the uncertainty which can arise in the application of grammatical knowledge to real texts. For example, definitions of abstract and concrete nouns in linguistic textbooks appear reasonably clear cut, but in practice the distinction between the two is less certain. Linguists have little difficulty accepting this uncertainty, and indeed they frequently relish the linguistic conversation the uncertainty can inspire: but for students it serves to confirm their view that not only is grammar difficult but it is also slippery.

Furthermore, there are some difficulties in acquiring grammatical knowledge which are caused by the specific characteristics of the grammar of English. Foremost amongst these is word class mobility, or functional shift: the way a single word in English is not always the same word class every time it is used. With the loss over time of many inflections in English, word morphology now gives relatively few clues about word class, and it is function within a syntactical unit which is the stronger clue. Postgraduate students, like learners of English grammar in school, often allow the most usual word class function of a word to dominate their interpretation (Myhill 2000). They temporarily lift the word from its context and think of its apparent verbal qualities or its noun qualities. For example, in analysing the persuasive features of an article, campaigning for the rights of refugee children, the noun phrase, 'the refugee child' caused some difficulty because students could remove the word 'refugee' from the phrase and identify it as a noun, rather than as a modifier as it is in context. Likewise, the phrase 'exploding shells' prompted many students to lift 'exploding' out of its context and perceive its verbal, active qualities and identify it as a verb. Indeed, participles and nouns functioning as adjectives frequently create this kind of confusion.

Similarly, the verb in English is perhaps the most versatile and flexible word class, and it is the grammatical unit which is often the driving force in a sentence. But this versatility, partially enabled by the limited number of inflections carried by the verb, can make it a difficult word class to grasp. The infinitive can look exactly the same as the finite form (to walk; I walk), and distinguishing between the past tense and the past participle is often confounded by identical forms (I walked; I had walked). Finite verbs change to indicate person, number and tense but modal verbs, which are always finite, do not change to show person or number. The main verb in a verb group is not always finite (I had been walking). Add to this the word class mobility noted above (the walk; my walking stick) and it is easy to see why the verb can be a challenge to even academically able learners. Moreover, a secure understanding of finite and non-finite verbs is a prerequisite to confident understanding of clause structure and this highlights another difficulty – so much grammatical understanding relies on other grammatical understandings. To understand a metaphor, you do not need to understand simile or alliteration: to understand a noun phrase, you need to understand not only the noun, but also premodifiers, determiners, post-modifiers, relative clauses and so on. The inter-connectedness of learning grammar is inevitable, but the cognitive challenge it poses should be acknowledged.

Dr Debra Myhill, Tutor for PGCE English students, School of Education, Exeter University

Appendix 2: grammar survey (see Chapter 2)

Student sheet

Below you will find 20 sentences written by English students learning German.

There is one mistake (underlined) in each sentence.

Can you think of a grammar rule or an explanation that would help the student to avoid this mistake?

Write your explanation in the table. If you can't think of anything, write N in the space.

Then write the correct form of the underlined phrase next to your explanation.

Item	Incorrect text	Correction	Grammar rule
1	Er besucht der alte Mann		
2	Ich habe mein Freundin getroffen		
3	Viele mein Freunde haben ein Auto		
4	Wir reden über allem Mögliche		
5	Ich helfe meine Mutter bei der Arbeit		
6	Eigentlich ich trinke kein Bier		
7	… wenn das Wetter schön ist		
8	Ich bin eine Zeitlang in der Fabrik gearbeitet		
9	Die anderen fahren weg früh am Morgen		
10	Ein kaltes Bier schmeckt besser wie ein warmes		
11	Sie ist nicht zu Wien gefahren		

Advanced Pathfinder 5: *Getting to grips with grammar* – 83

12	Ich <u>bin</u> seit Weihnachten arbeitslos gewesen
13	Er ist durch <u>der</u> Stadt gelaufen
14	Ich fahre niemals <u>bei</u> dem Flugzeug
15	Darf ich <u>Sie</u> ein kleines Geschenk geben?
16	Ich habe den ganzen Tag <u>müssen arbeiten</u>
17	<u>Was</u> Haus verkauft er?
18	<u>Wie</u> ist da? Mein Freund Klaus
19	Ich wasche <u>mich</u> jeden Abend die Haare.
20	Wenn ich Geld <u>hatte</u>, würde ich viel reisen.

Grammar survey analysis sheet

Categories of correct answer for grammar rule

(a) Item corrected + rule accurately expressed in technical language.
(b) Item corrected + rule expressed inaccurately or in colloquial terms.
(c) Item corrected but rule given is incorrect or 'N' (no rule) given.

Categories of incorrect answer for grammar rule

(d) Item incorrect but rule is correct if properly applied.
(e) Item incorrect + a rule correctly expressed but is not applicable.
(f) Item incorrect and 'N' given for rule, i.e. no answer available.
(g) Item wrongly corrected + wrong rule applied or inadequate explanation.
(h) 'N' + 'N' (no entries in either column).

Items containing errors		Correction OK	Grammar rule
1	Masculine accusative singular		
2	Feminine of possessive adjective		
3	Genitive plural of possessive after *viele*		
4	Accusative case after *über*		
5	Verb (*helfen*) taking dative		
6	Word order in main clause		

7	(word order after *wenn* in subordinate clause)
8	Correct auxiliary *haben* in perfect tense
9	Position of separable prefix *weg*
10	Use of *als* after comparative adjective
11	Use of preposition *nach* for places
12	Use of present tense with *seit*
13	Accusative case after *durch*
14	Use of preposition *mit* for modes of transport
15	Indirect object pronoun with *geben*
16	Word order modal verb in perfect tense
17	Correct interrogative adjective *welches?*
18	Correct interrogative pronoun *wer?*
19	Use of indirect object pronoun reflexive verbs
20	Use of subjunctive in conditional sentence

References

Belyaev, B. (1963) *The psychology of foreign language teaching.* Pergamon.

Borg, S. (1998) 'Talking about grammar in the language classroom'. In: *Language Awareness,* Vol. 7: 4, pp159–175.

Dept of Education and Science (1988) *National Curriculum report – English for ages 5–11* (Cox Report). HMSO.

DfEE (2001) *Framework for teaching English: Years 7, 8 and 9.* DfEE.

DfES (2002) *Qualifying to teach, professional standards for qualified teacher status and requirements for initial teacher training.* DfES.

Ellis, G. & Sinclair, B. (1989) *Learning to learn English.* Cambridge University Press.

Ellis, R. (2001) 'Investigating form-focused instruction'. In: *Language learning,* Vol. 51, Supplement 1, pp1–46.

Green, P. S. & Hecht, K. H. (1992) 'Implicit and explicit grammar: an empirical study'. In: *Applied linguistics,* Vol. 13, No. 2. Oxford University Press.

Hawkins, E. (1984) *Awareness of language: an introduction.* Cambridge University Press.

HMSO (1988) *Report of the committee of inquiry into the teaching of the English language* (Kingman Report). HMSO.

Jakobovits, L. A. (1970) *Foreign language learning.* Rowley, Mass.: Newbury House.

Johnson, K. (1988) 'Mistake correction'. In: *ELT Journal,* Vol. 42/2, pp89–95.

Johnstone, R. (1994) 'Grammar: acquisition and use'. In: King, L. & Boakes, P. (eds) *Grammar! A conference report.* CILT.

Jones, B. (2001) Advanced Pathfinder 2: *Developing learning strategies.* CILT.

Kelly, L. G. (1976) *25 centuries of language teaching*, Rowley, Mass.: Newbury House.

Krashen, S. (1985), *The input hypothesis: issues and implications.* Longman.

L'Huilier, M. , Martin, B. & Udris, R. (2000) *French discourse analysis*, Dublin: Philomel Productions Ltd.

Legutke, M. (1993) 'Room to talk', experiential learning in the foreign language classroom'. In: *Die neueren Sprachen,* Heft 4, pp319–323. Frankfurt: Diesterweg.

Little, D. (1994) 'Autonomy in language learning; some practical and theoretical considerations'. In: Swarbrick (1994), pp81–87.

Martin, J.-P. (1985) *Zum Aufbau didaktischer Teilkompetenzen beim Schüler.* Fremdsprachenunterricht auf der Basis des Informationsverarbeitungsansatzes. Tübingen: Narr.

Martin, J.-P. (1994) *'Grundlegende Gedanken von Jean-Pol Martin zu Lernen durch Lehren (LDL)'.* In: Graef, R. et al *Lernen durch Lehren.* Rimbach: Verlag im Wald.

McLachlan, A. (2001) Advanced Pathfinder 1: *Advancing oral skills.* CILT.

McLachlan, A. (2002) New Pathfinder 1: *Raising the standard.* CILT.

Mohammed, A. M. (1995) 'Grammar instruction in language development: rationale and technique'. In: *Language awareness*, Vol. 4:1, pp49–57.

Myhill, D. (2000) 'Misconceptions and difficulties in the acquisition of metalinguistic knowledge'. In: *Language and Education*, Vol. 14: 3, pp151–163.

Neather, E. (1989) 'Cognitive distance between languages and a differential approach to grammar'. In: *The place of grammar in language teaching and learning*, pp25–32. Paris: Didier.

Neather, E. (2001) Advanced Pathfinder 3: *Tests and targets.* CILT.

Nuffield Foundation (2000) *Languages: the next generation.* Oxford.

Nuttall, C. (1982) *Teaching reading skills in a foreign language.* Heinemann.

Reed, C. (2001) 'How attainable is AS?'. In: *Times Educational Supplement,* 15th June 2001, p5 of Modern Languages Supplement.

Rendall, H. (1998) Pathfinder 33: *Stimulating grammatical awareness.* CILT.

Rutherford. W. E. (1987) *Second language grammar: learning and teaching.* Longman.

Schmidt, R. W. (1990) 'The role of consciousness in second language learning'. In: *Applied Linguistics*, Vol. 11: 2, pp129–153.

Swarbrick, A. (ed) (1994) *Teaching modern languages.* Routledge.

Ur, P. (1988) *Grammar practice activities.* Cambridge University Press.

Ur, P. (1996) *A course in language teaching.* Cambridge University Press.

Widdowson, H. G. (1978) *Teaching language as communication.* Oxford University Press

advAnced
Pathfinder

The *Advanced Pathfinder* series promotes good advanced level language teaching and provides reference on key issues of concern, in particular those highlighted by requirements of the latest specifications. It presents ideas and practical guidance to motivate, interest and challenge students.

Series editor: Ted Neather

1 Advancing oral skills — *Anneli McLachlan*

2 Developing learning strategies — *Barry Jones*

3 Tests and targets — *Ted Neather*

4 Managing coursework — *Colin Christie*